LIFE DISRUPTED

Meg!
Thanks for your
friendship +
support!
XO, Tracy

LIFE DISRUPTED

FINDING YOUR WAY
FORWARD WHEN THE WORLD
IS UPSIDE DOWN

TRACY E. BALDWIN

NEW DEGREE PRESS

LIFE DISRUPTED
Finding Your Way Forward When the World Is Upside Down

ISBN   979-8-88504-640-4   Paperback
         979-8-88504-958-0   Kindle Ebook
         979-8-88504-845-3   Ebook

For the one who needs to read this. I wrote this for you.

Contents

---

*For a righteous man may fall
seven times, and rise again.*

—PROVERBS 24:16A NLT

Introduction

Where do you go when you are stuck in a dark place and you have given up on yourself? How do you gather the strength to carry on and get to a better place?

This book is a roadmap of how I did just that.

COVID-19 plays a big role in my book. It's what pushed me over the edge, and it's what's infecting me now as I finish this book (poetic perhaps, but not fun). However, the book isn't about COVID-19. It's about how to find your way forward when the world is upside down. Everyone, at some point in their life, feels that their world is a bit upside down. Mine was rocked by the pandemic.

The ripple effects of COVID-19 are only just beginning to be understood. The virus directly impacted millions of people who suffered after it first appeared in late December 2019 and spread around the globe. Most of them lived, but too many died, over six million as of this writing. Then there's the economic and social impact—and the mental toll.

Speaking of the mental toll, one of the symptoms of anxiety, as defined by the Anxiety and Depression Association of America, is having a sense of impending danger, panic, or doom. I'd wager a large part of adults in the US—and likely most of the planet—felt that way at some point during the pandemic, especially in the early days.

According to the Kaiser Family Foundation, by the end of January 2021, about a year into the pandemic, 41.5 percent of US adults were reporting symptoms of anxiety or depressive disorder. In 2019, before the world changed forever, only one in ten adults reported these symptoms (Panchal, 2021).

If you're a woman, your odds were worse. Even before the pandemic, women were nearly twice as likely as men to be diagnosed with an anxiety disorder in their lifetime (Harvard Medical School, 2007).

I am one of them.

I've been living with generalized anxiety disorder (GAD) since 2005, a condition I was successfully managing prior to the pandemic—until I wasn't.

Ten months into "work from home," I was feeling more and more like a trapped, scared animal that needed to escape from the urban confines of my shelter. As someone who struggles with claustrophobia and as a working mom of two teens and a tween, juggling my job and remote learning left me with a crushing feeling in my chest. I was constantly navigating the evolving rules of learning and working in this new normal. I was extremely irritable and on edge.

It is for those who may have been high achievers all their lives, trying to be perfect, more productive, and the best they could be until they just couldn't anymore.

This is for those who struggle with anxiety and depression and ask themselves if they can ever be "normal."

This is for those in the next generation of women: my sister, my daughters, my nieces, and beyond. I hope it offers support and a roadmap to weather the storms of life and achieve their dreams.

This book is also for me too, as it has helped me process what happened.

We owe it to ourselves to live our most authentic life with love, hope, and courage—not hate, despair, and shame. Our time on Earth is short.

I hope it inspires you to face your fears and walk through life fully present. To do this, you will need the support of your body, mind, and soul. But you can't do it alone! You need other humans and spiritual energy.

My hope is this book can be one of the tools to help you stand back up when you get knocked down or prevent you from falling down in the first place. (You will still get knocked around, just not knocked down or out.)

PART ONE

THE STOP SIGN

CHAPTER 1

Stop Signs

———

"There will come a time when you believe everything is finished; that will be the beginning."

— LOUIS L'AMOUR

Stop signs are a pause in a journey. The semicolons in life. Some are unique. Some are not. But we all have them.

It's the unexpected, when hope seems absent: the devastating diagnosis, the breakup, the job loss, the miscarriage, the sudden death of a loved one.

It can also be the expected, when hope seems abundant: the first day of school, graduation, the first job, marriage, having children.

Some stop signs happen whether we like it or not. Some may halt you in your tracks rather than allow a rolling stop. They may knock you down, take the wind out of your sails. These are the ones that radically change the trajectory of your life.

SNOWSTORMS AND SARAH SILVERMAN

The day I unexpectedly hit one of the hardest stop signs in my fifty-year road trip on Earth was also the day Chicago experienced a "significant snowfall event." It was significant in meteorological terms, as we recorded 10.3 inches of snow in a twenty-four- to thirty-hour period. It was the most snowfall at once in five years, and the month was the tenth snowiest January on record.

The snow in the Midwest can be heavy and wet and come down in big, sticky flakes. It can also be light and airy. Either way, it accumulates in huge drifts in inconvenient places, such as narrow alleys lined with garages and garbage containers.

This particular snowstorm started on a Saturday and ended Sunday morning, January 31, 2021, at the precise moment I most needed it.

I had struggled with anxiety on and off for a little over fifteen years—truthfully, probably most of my life. It rears its ugly head when I take on too many tasks and face a huge amount of uncertainty. It manifests as panic attacks, claustrophobia, not wanting to get out of bed, sleeping all the time, or all of the above.

I was struggling again. My anxiety was amplified by the uncertainty and stress of a global pandemic—a city and nation on edge and politically divided, remote work, remote school, dealing with two teens who were struggling with mental health and schoolwork, navigating the unknown. I was trying to hold it all together, feeling like one more thing could push me over the edge.

My job has been a respite for me—a place I could control and excel. I have always been a high performer, recognized and rewarded for my work my entire career. Until one Friday afternoon, when I was blindsided. My performance was abruptly and unjustly called into question. The dread I was constantly feeling from the pandemic, my toxic workplace, and life, in general, came to a boiling point. I crashed, broke, and spiraled downward.

On Saturday the snow started outside, covering the city, and inside, it clouded my mind. Heavy thoughts floated downward and covered the common sense synapses firing in my brain.

Then came Sunday.

You see, that morning, I was in a sad, hopeless, distressed, and dark place. I needed to escape my bedroom, my house, and my life. It is not a place anyone wants to be and is a place that borders on delirium and desperation. During "normal" times, pre-pandemic, I maybe could have pulled myself together. But the stifling unknown made me feel like a trapped animal. My fight-or-flight system kicked in; I wanted to flee and just disappear.

So I took off with my keys and purse, disheveled in my flannel pajamas and down coat, not knowing where I was going to go. I was just going to drive. I wasn't sure where, but I didn't want to come back.

I passed my ten-year-old daughter on the way out of the house, who innocently asked, "Where are you going?" I honestly replied, "I don't know," as I stormed out the sliding glass door through the back, stomped through the newly fallen snow, and forced my way to our standalone garage. I opened the side door and immediately turned to push the button to open the lumbering, two-car garage door.

The eerie silence that happens after a fresh snow greeted me, soon broken by the sound of neighbors clearing snow with their muscles and machines. I grabbed a shovel and started to dig a path through two feet of snow so I could get my car out. After twenty minutes or so of furious work, I had cleared enough of a path to get my giant minivan out of the garage. I knew in my bones I could probably not make it out of the garage, let alone clear the alley—but I was mad, determined, and not in my right mind.

I fired up the minivan and forced the family truckster out of its comfortable cave into the frozen tundra. I made it past two houses before I got stuck—really stuck. When you are on your way to the point of no return, this is frustrating. I was failing. Mother Nature and Jack Frost had teamed up against me to foil my plan.

A few of my middle-aged male neighbors gallantly came to shovel out the damsel in distress. One of them simply offered, "Do you need some help?" I nodded my head yes and then sat stone-faced in my delirium in the driver's seat, gunning the gas, swerving the wheels, shifting from reverse to drive, reverse to drive, as they picked at the snow with their shovels and salt. We all worked together, mostly in silence except for the sound of the wheels spinning in the snow and the engine revving to free me.

I was about two car lengths from leaving the alley and reaching the side street. Even if I was able to get unstuck and make it that far, it was abundantly clear, I wouldn't be able to drive down the street until the city snowplows could clear the way. Realistically, that could be two or three days. The only way out was to go back to where I started, whether I liked it or not, and make a plan B.

My husband was among the knights who shoveled me out. I could tell he thought I was being melodramatic and the others thought I was a crazy, dim-witted woman trying to get out in a minivan—a minivan!—post-storm when there was literally no chance of that happening. They didn't say it out loud, but their faces betrayed them.

Once I was free, I had to throw the gray whale into reverse and back slowly into the garage—back to where I started. I don't know how much time had passed—maybe an hour, maybe two.

But I still wasn't in a good frame of mind. My husband demanded to know what the heck I was doing after the car was safely back in the garage. "Where did you think you were going?" he asked, six inches from my face once I was out of the car and standing next to him.

I defiantly replied, a mix of anger and defeat blazing from my eyes, "I don't know, but I just wanted to get away from here and not come back." I then turned on my heels, marched back into the house, up the stairs and into my room, and slammed the door.

I plopped on my bed, and started to conjure up a plan B: Pills? I got up, went to the bathroom, and grabbed the bottle of Xanax out of my medicine cabinet. I stared at it and decided I didn't have enough to put me into an eternal slumber, so I just took one.

Back to bed, I grabbed my phone and googled "how to kill yourself." That brought me to the suicide hotline. I didn't want to talk to anyone. Then I ended up on Instagram.

Sarah Silverman, the American comedian, popped up in my feed. Born in December 1970, she is six months older than me and has struggled with depression. She had the intriguing question, "Thinking about killing yourself?" So I thought, *Why yes, I was. How did she know? Was it some sort of Facebook algorithm that was reading my mind? What did she have to say?* I clicked on the video and listened.

She told me she thought it was a bad idea (which I expected). But then she went on to tell me I was a procrastinator most likely (I was), and so why not today, of all days, procrastinate and put your plans off for one day?

I thought long and hard about it, and thought, *Yes, I could probably put my plans off for one day and choose to procrastinate this one task, as I had so many others in my life. This one would potentially be one that would be infinitely final. So yes, I could do this. I could procrastinate one more time.*

I could take a little more time at my stop sign and wait.

I laid there in bed, looking up at the sky-blue painted walls that surrounded a sloped, sixteen-foot bright white ceiling in my bedroom and the two skylights providing a glimpse into a gray, snowy heaven, where I so desperately wanted to go. I was so sad. So defeated. So tired.

How did I get here? I didn't even know. I gave up trying to figure it out. But at that moment, I didn't give up on life. Instead, I closed my eyes, and fell into a fitful sleep, exhausted by the morning's battle.

THE FINE LINE

When you hit a stop sign as I did on January 31, 2021, you feel helpless, trapped in the dark, and lonely. My mind was numb. I was scared. Ashamed. Sad. I knew I needed help. And it had to be more than my therapist, who I had spoken to in an emergency Zoom call (thanks telehealth) that fateful Sunday morning at 9 a.m.

I was such a mess after the call that morning before trying to make my ill-fated escape. Delirious. Hopeless. I felt so low, I had to stop the pain in any way possible. I felt like I was literally going to jump out of my skin. My desire to run as far away as possible was blocked by a record snowstorm and a comedian. Another thing helped: a text I received from my therapist after our call.

"You can do hard things," she had typed.

Those words penetrated my psychotic fog and were like a lighthouse flashing in my mind. *You can do hard things, you can do hard things.*

But was it harder to leave or stay? I decided it was to stay. I had to stay. For me. For my family.

Thousands of people have those thoughts every year. In fact, suicide was the tenth leading cause of death for adults in America in 2019 according to the Centers for Disease Control and Prevention (CDC), with over 47,000 people in the United States dying by suicide, and 1.3 million attempting it. More and more people have had these thoughts recently, with the rate of suicide increasing every year since 2006. The good news is that it is totally preventable.

Knowing the risk factors and recognizing the warning signs for suicide can help prevent suicide. The CDC reports that firearms are the most common method of death, used in more than half of all suicides. According to the Suicide Awareness Voices of Education, among the risk factors I was experiencing was feeling trapped and hopeless. I was also extremely anxious and agitated, and about to be reckless.

I'm glad I didn't have access to a firearm. I had a snowstorm and Sarah Silverman.

In moments like these, between life and death, there is an exceptionally tiny fine line. It is a choice. Do I stay, or do I go? Do I give up, or give in to the pain? It is a choice one makes in an especially vulnerable moment. People like Robin Williams, Kate Spade, and Anthony Bourdain came to mind, along with others I personally knew. Are these the questions they had before they crossed?

What can we learn from these tragedies? I'm hoping one lesson is: We need to destigmatize mental health issues. Another is: We should all be aware of the warning signs of suicide and know what to do if we see them. For those like me who deal with anxiety, reassure them, teach them, and give them the space to be broken or ask for help.

I need to remind myself, and others like me, that desperation is like a wave in the ocean. It rises and then crashes on the shore, eventually subsiding. Those, like me, who travel down that dark path need a reason, whether big or small, to let the moment pass. Because the hard and wonderful truth is that it does. The moment does pass. To a time where you are on more solid ground and your mind is a little more clear. We all need a tiny stone, or bridge, to step on, to get us to the next moment to hold on. The universe, or God, or both, gave me a few.

TURNING THE PAGE
I have since learned emotions are energy in motion. Emotions come and go. They are temporary. They pass in and out of us or sometimes get stuck. Thankfully, my wave of desperation to escape subsided in my ocean of despair long enough for me to swim to the shore.

Maybe the stop sign you came to was different, or maybe it was the same, but either way, you stopped. Life came to a screeching halt. Maybe the bottom dropped out. A death.

An illness. A breakup. A job loss. Some disappointment that caught you by surprise.

Or maybe it was another milestone, like someone graduating high school, or college, or moving to another town for a job, a marriage, a child. It could be something that brings you joy. It's not disappointing, but it causes you to reevaluate who you are and your role in life.

The page gets turned, and it's a new chapter. It's a natural pause. Do you continue as you are, or do you adjust who you are? I knew I had to move forward and make adjustments to my life. I needed to be better prepared for the next time I fell in the valley.

Jessie Van Amburg, a freelance writer and editor, quit her job during the pandemic. Like millions of Americans, she suffered from burnout, which, as defined by the World Health Organization, is an occupational phenomenon caused by unsuccessfully managing chronic work stress. It leaves a person physically and emotionally drained and negatively impacts work performance. She, along with 84 percent of her fellow millennials, had been suffering pre-pandemic. But she at least had the help of a therapist to cope.

When the pandemic happened, she wrote, "Overnight, my life shrunk to contain only what was inside my eight-hundred-square foot Brooklyn apartment: my household (my fiancé and our cats), and work. I was deeply fortunate to still have a job, much less a place to live. But with nothing else enriching my life—no time with friends, no visits to my family in California, no outdoor space (save a fire escape)—there was nothing else to balance out the relentless demands of my job. It took me a long time to realize that this wasn't normal or healthy, that I wouldn't feel better with a week off, or at the end of the month."

She did some reevaluation of her priorities with her therapist and determined she needed to quit her job and find a different path. She made adjustments to her life, including recalibrating her budget and scheduling a courthouse wedding with her fiancé so she could get his health insurance. Then she took the leap.

She reported, "That first Monday, I woke up about as euphoric as a twenty-something at a Harry Styles concert. FedExing back my work laptop felt like exorcising a stress demon from my body. I've been sleeping better (as long as my cat doesn't wake me up at 5 a.m.), and I finally have time to enjoy things I love, like reading and gardening. I'm doing some freelance writing to help pay the bills and agonizing over the outline of what I'm hoping could be my first novel. While I still struggle with depression—and get tired and overwhelmed more easily than I used to—I'm slowly starting to feel more like myself than I have in years."

She concluded, she "might still be charred at the edges from my burnout, but I'm healing every day. And that's worth more to me than any job title in the world."

For me, my first step to the rest of my life was clearing some time and space to refocus. That was hard in the cramped confines of my home where I had been working for ten months with my husband while my three children went to school remotely.

I didn't feel well enough to go back to work. I spoke with my healthcare team and a few lawyer friends about my options. They let me know I could take a leave of absence, for up to three months, using the Family and Medical Leave Act (FMLA). I was familiar with FMLA from my past maternity leaves. According to the US Department of Labor, FMLA entitles eligible employees to take unpaid, job-protected leave for specified family and medical reasons. It guarantees the continuation of group health insurance coverage under the same terms and conditions as if the employee had not taken leave.

So I was able to take time from work to get in a better mental space and have health insurance and the caretakers I needed to help me.

My friends and family expressed doubt that I could do such a thing (FMLA for mental health?), but my therapist, executive coach, and lawyer friends assured me it was a real thing, and more and more people were seeking help during the pandemic.

I didn't go back to work after that fateful Friday. I took the week off, and then eleven more, to complete the FMLA.

After I got the help I needed initially, I started to create my own recovery plan. I really wanted to fly my cuckoo's nest to a hospital to convalesce but those weren't realistic options.

COVID-19 made travel next to impossible; besides, my family needed me. Financially, we wouldn't be able to swing it.

But I desperately wanted to get better and not feel this way anymore.

Requesting the FMLA leave was one of the scariest things I had to do in my career. *What would other people think? Would this hurt my career? What if future employers found out?* I pushed aside my fear and did it. It turned out to be one of the best things I ever did.

Once I was granted the time away and the FMLA was approved, I was determined to make the most of my time. I really wanted to find a quiet place I could go to for an extended time to reflect and heal from what had just happened. I fantasized about going to a convent, like Maria von Trapp in *Sound of Music* did before she found the Captain and her job as a nanny in Austria so many years ago. But that wasn't realistic or even possible since I had three children and a husband. Should I check myself into an inpatient facility? That also didn't seem feasible. It was about four days after the snowstorm. I didn't think I was an active threat to myself anymore, as the feeling of impending doom had passed, and I felt like I was given a temporary reprieve to figure things out. I was still raw from everything, though, and wasn't quite ready to go back to life. But I didn't want to go backward, and still felt like I was on a slippery slope.

I knew I just had to stop. Stop life to the best of my ability and reassess. So I did—with the time I had, up to twelve weeks, and resources in my toolbox, including professionals like my therapist and primary care physician, people in my personal life like a few close friends and my husband, and God. It seemed like a mountain, but I knew it was a journey I had to take. I was scared, depleted of energy, almost lifeless. My only option was one step at a time.

I have to admit, it's a little easier to disappear from work when you are remote and don't have to face anyone. No one really knows you are missing or misses you except a select few. None of your friends or family really know as you are all in quarantine, just trying to make it. Everyone is remote and in hiding.

Stopping saved me. It allowed me to take time to reflect on why my mind was fried and my body wanted to escape. It was a much-needed time-out.

When we hit a stop sign and sink to the lowest of lows—or feel like life is in a freefall—the first step we need to take is to decide to take a first step. Grab onto something. Look for the helpers. Eventually, we will rise up again.

CHAPTER 1 QUESTIONS:

1. Have you hit a stop sign in your life? What was it? What feelings did you experience when it happened? How did you move past it?

2. Have you ever experienced work-related burnout? How did you get past it? If you are still in a "chronically stressful work environment," what tactics do you employ to cope with it?

3. Do you believe emotions are energy in motion? Why or why not? What do you think happens to us when emotions get stuck?

4. How is mental health viewed in the workplace? What additional support can be provided?

5. How can we as individuals and/or society support people who feel suicidal?

CHAPTER 2

No Man Is an Island

---

*No man is an island, Entire of itself; Every man is a piece of
the continent, A part of the main.*

— JOHN DONNE

So what does rock bottom look like for someone suffering
from anxiety or depression? For me, it was a deep, dark pit
with massive, seemingly infinite walls. You may hear the
world going on around you, even see shards of light—but you
are in solitary confinement of your own making.

My hard stop, my breakdown, left me numb. I barely moved
and went through the motions of living. I knew I wasn't
okay, and I needed help. I knew I couldn't dig out of where
I was by myself. So I took the first step by asking for help
and accepting it.

This was a lesson I learned early in life. My parents divorced
when I was four. I lived with my mom and little brother in a
ranch-style house in the suburbs of Chicago. It was referred
to as a "bedroom community." There was no industry around,

just single-family homes that sprung up in former farm fields and the businesses and schools needed to support them.

My first day of kindergarten was on the horizon. It was only a half-day, as it was in the 1970s. Most moms still didn't work outside of the home, but as a single mom, mine did. She had arranged for another mom in the neighborhood to watch my baby brother and me. The weekend before school started, we practiced walking from the elementary school, around the corner, and a few blocks to the babysitter's house.

The big day arrived. I was so excited to start school, learn, and meet new friends. I was a little nervous about my walk after school, but I was a big girl now and thought I could handle it.

The time flew by. Before I knew, the class was over. I walked through the playground with my classmates. I chatted with them as, one by one, they went home with their parents. I stood frozen at the school ground gate, not remembering which way to turn. After all the parents and children had come and gone, I was alone.

After what seemed like an eternity to my five-year-old mind, I made the choice to go left out of the school instead of right. I was soon very, very lost.

I was wandering around the neighborhood, crying when a middle-aged kind man working in his garage saw me. "Hey there," he called out to me. "Is everything okay?" he asked.

"No," I whimpered. "I'm lost," I told him. I broke down in tears. "Today was my first day of school and I don't know how to get to my babysitter's house."

He put down what he was working on in the garage and took my hand. "Everything is going to be alright," he reassured me as he patted my hand. "Let's go back to the school and retrace your steps." It sounded like a good plan to me, as my current situation wasn't working.

We eventually found our way to our babysitter's house. She didn't seem too bothered I was missing for so long—as it had just occurred to her that I should have been back. I didn't know much in my few years of life thus far, but I did know adults were inconsistent. I could trust some, but not others. Until I could figure out which was which, I knew I needed to take care of myself. I made a vow at that time to pay closer attention to everything and try not to make any mistakes like that again.

As sad as that story is to me, it is also one of hope. One man helped me find my way back home. Mr. Rogers shared his mother's advice about what to tell children when they are afraid of what they see on the news or in the movies. "Always look for the helpers. There will always be helpers…. If you look for the helpers, you'll know that there's hope." I did that day, and then decades later, remembered that piece of advice again. I needed to look for helpers. I couldn't find my way back alone.

At the same time, that experience seared into my brain I had to do what I could to take care of myself. I never wanted to feel lost and scared like that again. I learned to be independent and not to rely on others for my well-being. That independent streak has served me well for most of my life, until it didn't.

That's been one of the key fault lines zigzagging through my life—knowing when to look for and ask for help and when to go it alone. I've always leaned more into the myth of the Lone Ranger to survive as the years went by, like many Americans born before the millennium. Individualism is a sacred character trait that is part of our country's DNA—for better or for worse. It was a learned response from my experience in kindergarten. Even at that time, I innately knew I couldn't find my way back alone, so I sought help. I trusted my inner voice, even though it was just a whisper.

Finding my way back to wellness after the cold day in January 2021 more than forty-four years later, I knew in the depths of my soul I couldn't do it alone.

THE POEM
At the other end of my public school adventure, I learned another valuable lesson. I was a senior in high school. In my humanities class, where we read literature from different cultures around the world, we identified the values that made us uniquely human despite geography and time.

In class, we explored different themes about the collective human spirit. We discussed how people need people—we aren't meant to live alone, we need each other to thrive, and we are all connected. This was a new idea to me, as I had been fiercely independent until that point. We reviewed the seventeenth-century English author John Donne's poem, "No Man Is an Island."

We had to memorize it for a grade. I dutifully completed the assignment, but I didn't fully understand its meaning until recently.

NO MAN IS AN ISLAND

No man is an island,
Entire of itself;
Every man is a piece of the continent,
A part of the main.
If a clod be washed away by the sea,
Europe is the less,
As well as if a promontory were:
As well as if a manor of thy friend's
Or of thine own were.
Any man's death diminishes me,
Because I am involved in mankind.
And therefore never send to know for whom the bell tolls;
It tolls for thee.

This poem has stayed with me ever since I came across it in the late 1980s. It has taken on more meaning with age. At the time, I felt "the collective" was my friends, as a teenager might. Now, since I've gotten older and have become an active citizen in my city, state, and country, I see the larger society outside of high school. I understand how it talks about the greater good, how we are all connected, and that actions of one impact the well-being of all.

It has helped shape my political beliefs, as well as my personal and professional beliefs. We are all better when we acknowledge and participate in the collective. The times I've tried to do things on my own have been disastrous to me, and I'd argue the collective. Even today, as I write this, the US is experiencing an epidemic of mass shootings due to assault rifles in the wrong hands. I see how this poem resonates with a universal human truth that society collectively is choosing to ignore. We are paying for it dearly.

Poets aren't the only ones who say people need people. Scientists say it too. Social connection is a pillar of lifestyle medicine (Martino, 2017). In fact, research shows low social interaction was reported to be similar to smoking fifteen cigarettes a day and to being an alcoholic, to be more harmful than not exercising, and to be twice as harmful as obesity.

Bottom line: we are wired to connect with others. When we do, it impacts us positively, and when we don't there are negative repercussions to our health.

An article in the November–December 2017 issue of the *American Journal of Lifestyle Medicine* explained, "From psychological theories to recent research, there is significant evidence that social support and feeling connected can help people maintain a healthy body mass index, control blood sugars, improve cancer survival, decrease cardiovascular mortality, decrease depressive symptoms, mitigate post-traumatic stress disorder symptoms, and improve overall mental health. The opposite of connection, social isolation, has a negative effect on health and can increase depressive symptoms as well as mortality."

In other words, loneliness can kill.

What this means to me is when you are at the darkest depths or the highest highs, you need people. They help pull you up out of darkness or at least walk alongside you and hold space for you. If you are experiencing joy, it is even sweeter if you can share it with someone else. These human connections are the essence of being human. As it turns out, it directly impacts your health—like vitamins, food, water, or sunlight.

Research study after research study shows people who have solid relationships are more content and live longer. The Harvard Study of Adult Development, the longest study of its kind with more than eighty years of research, found "close relationships, more than money or fame, are what keep people happy throughout their lives." In addition, "the ties protect people from life's discontents, help to delay mental and physical decline, and are better predictors of long and happy lives than social class, IQ, or even genes. That finding proved true across the board among both the Harvard men and the inner-city participants" (Mineo, 2017).

The latest director of the study, Robert Waldinger, said in a TED Talk that's been viewed more than forty-two million times, "The people who were the most satisfied in their relationships at age fifty were the healthiest at age eighty." Researchers also found those with strong social support experienced less mental deterioration as they aged, and those with high marital satisfaction experienced better mental health.

When I was at my lowest moment, my husband was there. So was Sarah Silverman. I spoke to my therapist. My friends tried to cheer me up with flowers and hugs. I surrounded myself with people who believed in me.

KARIANNE'S STORY

Losing a pregnancy and a job in the same afternoon brought thirty-five-year-old Karianne Michelle's life to a screeching halt.

After learning her third painful attempt at in vitro fertilization had been unsuccessful, she received another phone call informing her that her position at the communications agency she worked at was eliminated. Of that difficult time in her life, she told me when I interviewed her in 2021, "As sad as I was, I thought that clearly, the universe was trying to tell me something."

A few months later, Karianne redirected her nurturing energy and put it toward creating another baby in January 2017: her own business, Lofti. She repurposed the marketing skills she used for her Fortune 100 clients to help small businesses and female entrepreneurs build their brands. But another stop sign was just around the corner.

Despite her new start with her business, she and her husband struggled in their marriage, and they got counseling. She thought things were getting better, but she was wrong.

When Karianne returned home one afternoon after visiting her brother in Washington, DC, she opened the door to a new life. The house was empty, and her husband of sixteen years and college sweetheart was gone without a trace.

Picking herself up after heartbreak, Karianne worked with a support team including her closest friends and a therapist. She leaned on them when she didn't believe in herself and suggested the same help for others facing adversity. "Surround yourself with people who believe in you, who see the best in you. My friends would tell me I was strong, and then give me examples of things I'd accomplished."

SANDY'S STORY

Surrounding yourself with people who believe in you can make all the difference. For some, quality over quantity really matters.

Sandy Marsico knows having the right people at your side can be the fuel that takes your belief in yourself to the next level. The female founder and owner of one of Chicago's best companies to work for, and one of the fastest-growing companies in America, Sandstorm Design, started her company shortly after she graduated from college.

While her tribe of supporters is large today, she didn't always feel the support of those closest to her. When she first started her business, Sandy's college boyfriend didn't buy into her dreams. "He would ask me, 'When are you going to get a job? I won't marry you until you make as much as me. You will never do that doing this thing that you're doing. You're not really working,'" she confided.

But it wasn't just him. "My friends were asking me when I was going to get a real job. However, I had one person believe in me outside of my mom, dad, and brother. One. Out of my entire friend group from college. But it just takes one to make a difference."

That one friend had similar dreams to Sandy—to start their own successful business. "He had huge aspirations and dreams to build a multimillion-dollar company. I had aspirations and dreams of just paying bills. He had a coach helping him develop his business plan. I had the bookstore and him encouraging me through every step of my start-up," she said.

When she told her parents she was starting a new business at age twenty-four, they said, "Sounds great. If it doesn't work out, you can move back home." She said, "They didn't tell me no. Or that I was crazy, or taking too big a risk, like many parents would have."

Sandy was so thankful her parents believed in her. "That was how they were able to support me. They didn't have money. They didn't have connections, nothing like that. But they said, 'You should go for it.' There was never a pause on the phone. Never did they question me or make me feel like I couldn't do it," she said. "When my mom was in the last year of her life, I straight up asked her. 'Now that I have kids, I need to know, did you worry about me?' And she said, 'Every day.'"

At age twenty-three, Sandy bought her first house after being turned down for a mortgage fourteen times, and at twenty-four she quit her job to start her company. She doesn't let losing clients or competitive pitches at her agency get her down. "I know eventually I'll win; I just have to keep trying."

When she met her husband, he believed so much in her and her company, he never complained about the late nights and weekends. Instead, he would stay up late with her and play video games or watch TV so she wasn't alone. "Having a life partner who could handle the intensity and energy of an entrepreneur was a game-changer," she said. "He took care of a thousand little things our family needed so I could focus on the company's growth." Sandstorm has continued to grow year-over-year ever since.

"I never thought I'd be among the 4 percent of small businesses in America who achieved $1 million in revenue, or the less than the one percent who surpass $5 million, but I did."

THE MYTH OF THE LONE RANGER

When someone achieves success in life, be it an actor or actress, musician, politician, athlete, or an entrepreneur like Sandy, we often focus our congratulations on the person and don't look beyond them when we give credit for their success. Unfortunately, we all—society, the media, and individuals—get fixated on the person. That's just the way we are wired, right?

Sure, the person who achieved their goal is part of their success, but they are not the entire reason for it. So much goes into that success. Often a whole team of people are behind that success—which is why the Academy Awards and other award ceremony speeches can seemingly drag on forever.

For Sandy, she has a company of forty-plus people to help her achieve her business goals. She also has an extended support system of family, friends, and other life helpers. Athletes have coaches, trainers, family, and friends. Actors have agents, personal trainers, acting coaches, stylists, nutritionists, friends and family, and so on.

But in America, we are known for our individualism. We have a Puritan, pull-yourself-up-by-your-bootstraps work ethic. We can do it alone. We are rewarded with accolades for doing it by ourselves.

The bootstrap metaphor is thought to have originated in 1834, in an NYC-based newspaper called *The Workingman's Advocate*, as a way to describe doing something that was seemingly impossible. Tech companies now use the term to refer to a set of self-sustaining processes. Startups adopt a "bootstrapping" strategy where they get by with little resources (money, people), and use a combination of hard work, smarts, and a little bit of luck to be successful.

Today, the legend of the bootstrapper and Lone Ranger myth have become entrenched in popular American culture, and perhaps even embedded in our country's DNA. Just look at the hundreds of movies and stories where the lone hero faces impossible odds, only to come out on top.

We hear about self-made success stories—people like Jeff Bezos. The myth is that he, and others like him, do it alone.

Jeff Bezos was born to a seventeen-year-old mom and eighteen-year-old dad who divorced eighteen months after Bezos was born when his mother was a senior in high school. After the divorce, they lived on her parent's ranch in New Mexico.

His grandfather taught him his work ethic, as did his stepdad, a non-English-speaking Cuban immigrant who married Bezos's mom when he was four (Quinn, 2022).

His stepdad, Miguel Bezos, adopted Jeff and went to and graduated from the same college as Jeff's mom. Jeff was inspired by his stepdad's struggles and said his family has been a key motivator and support in his life. "My dad came here from Cuba all by himself without speaking English when he was sixteen years old, and has been kicking ass ever since. Thank you for all the love and heart, Dad!" Jeff posted on Instagram on June 17, 2018, praising his father's grit and determination and thanking him for his support.

Jeff went onto college at Princeton, and then to his first job as a hedge fund manager in New York City where he met and married MacKenzie, an aspiring writer and administrative assistant. It was MacKenzie, now his ex-wife, who shared his love of books and encouraged him to leave his hedge fund job and move to Seattle to pursue his dream of starting an online bookstore. In fact, she wrote the company's first business plan and was its first accountant (Quinn, 2022).

"When you have loving and supportive people in your life, like [ex-wife] MacKenzie, my parents, my grandfather, my grandmother, you end up being able to take risks. Because I think it's one of those things, you know, you kind of know that somebody's got your back. And so if you're thinking about it logically, it's an emotional thing" (Dopfner, 2018).

When it came time to start to scale Amazon, Bezos had the support of twenty investors who each gave $50,000, including his parents who used their life savings, to help the company get the funding they needed (Rosoff, 2016). So no, Bezos did not get where he is today alone.

For me, the self-made success story was reinforced along the way during childhood, as I excelled in school despite coming from a broken home, being raised by divorced parents, despite being on food stamps at one time. If I had problems, I didn't let people know and tried to solve them on my own. I was a straight-A student and overachiever without anyone's help, and I was rewarded for it—until I wasn't.

When I reached the workplace, this overachiever was thrown into a new game with new rules. Despite all of my accomplishments and hard work, I was laid off three times in the course of my career for economic reasons. (Being a working mom, I sometimes thought that was an unsaid strike against me too.) Even though it wasn't my fault, I took these setbacks personally and didn't always know how to bounce back. I still believed in the myth of the Lone Ranger and the legend of the bootstrapper.

Losing my job was out of my control and that felt terrible. I needed help.

I sought that help from a therapist provided for me as part of the outsourcing tools from two of my layoffs. I received three visits as part of my EAP, or employee assistance program. The visits helped me reframe the situation and not take it so personally.

I also sought the help and support of my family and friends, like Bezos, who also reassured me of my worth, and reminded me life was more than any one job or career. These are the people who helped return me to center when I was feeling low and out of sorts.

In my role as a parent I also learned to ask for help. As a working mom of young children, I had to. The day did not have enough hours for me to be present for pick up and drop off at school or activities and everything in between. I needed a team to help me, which included my parents, friends, and caregivers.

But at work, it wasn't as easy, or as clear-cut on how to ask for help and from who. It seemed like a sign of weakness to ask for help—that I wasn't being "boot strappy" or working hard enough. I often didn't seek help because it might take too long to explain to someone else. Or it might be too costly. Or it might interrupt my flow and one crack in the armor would make it all fall apart. There are a million reasons I didn't and don't ask for help, and others don't ask for help.

SUPPORT SYSTEMS MATTER

Niro Feliciano, LCSW, writes in *This Book Won't Make You Happy* that connection is one of the eight keys to finding true contentment. In the chapter about connection, she shares a story about Ian Hockley, her friend and father of Dylan Hockley, one of the first graders killed in a mass shooting at Sandy Hook Elementary School in 2012. When she asked Ian what helped him get through the unthinkable for any parent, he had a one-word answer: "Friends." While he said the grief will never go away, his connection "with friends and a support system of relationships" has allowed him to find purpose and meaning in the midst of pain.

These support systems help people endure the stop signs in life—a devastating diagnosis, loss of a loved one, breakup, burnout, and breakdown.

Feliciano admits connecting can be hard given the fast pace and busyness of our lives. She wrote, "This busyness—and the lack of connection because of it—is the price of the 'more' that we constantly seek. But like with anything important, if we don't make the time, a deeper connection with others will never magically appear."

The point is you can't do it alone. We aren't meant to do it alone. Developing meaningful connections takes time and commitment. So who's on your team? How can you develop deeper relationships where you find connection? We'll explore more about how to identify the people and the tools to help keep you centered and resilient in Part Two.

During the pandemic, when faced with another out-of-my-control situation with life and work, I knew I couldn't do it by myself anymore. That's why I stopped and started on a new path, with the help of people and some new tools.

Maybe it was age or desperation, but I was ready for some additional help.

CHAPTER 2 QUESTIONS:

1. What does the poem "No Man Is an Island?" mean to you?

2. Did you know the quality of your relationships has a higher predictor of your health as you age than your cholesterol level? What is the quality of your most important relationships? How can they improve?

3. Do you have others who believe in you? Who are they? If you don't, where do you think you can find them?

4. When you have gone through hard times, who has been there for you?

5. Do you think the myth of the Lone Ranger or the legend of the bootstrapper are accurate? Why or why not?

6. How do you think women can be supported more at home and/or in the workplace?

CHAPTER 3

The Pandemic Flux

———

"Challenges are gifts that force us to search for a new center of gravity. Don't fight them. Just find a new way to stand."

— OPRAH WINFREY

When you go through a life transition or hit a stop sign, a lot of times you feel the urge to return to normal, or at least to find steadier ground.

I know I felt that way after that snowy January morning. Except I didn't want the old normal. I wanted a new normal— but I didn't know what that was. That unknown state can cause an anxious person to have more anxiety or a depressed person to be more depressed. But the good news is, humans— including me—are resilient. It's how we are built.

The truth of the matter is, there is no going back. The only way out is forward. "Onward!" as a friend of mine says.

Sometimes, a big change is unwanted—and that change causes anxiety. Ever since the world got infected by a spiky microscopic ball we now know as COVID-19, nothing has been the same. We hear phrases to describe this historic era as "unprecedented times" and that what comes next is "the new normal." But what is this "new normal"? It may bring good things and it may bring bad things—but when we continually face the unknown, it certainly causes a lot of anxiety.

It has impacted our life, our livelihoods, our home life, and our relationships. The spikes have wedged into the cracks of society and ripped open the scabs. As of October 2021, the pandemic was the third-leading cause of death in the United States behind heart disease and cancer and has killed more than 700,000 from the virus—more than the population of Boston. The ripple effects have been exponential (Ahmad and Anderson, 2021).

The US experienced the highest year-to-year increase in the murder rate in 2020 since national records started being kept in 1960 (MacFarquhar, 2021). The rise in murders roughly coincides with the eighteen months of the pandemic. Gun sales increased during this time too, with the FBI reporting more weekly background checks in 2020 and 2021 than any other year since they've kept records. More guns coupled with a pandemic can spell trouble.

Clinical psychologist Dr. Maria Espinola, who has worked in jails and juvenile centers, said, "People who witnessed violence at home or in their communities when they were growing up, and maybe have a genetic tendency to aggression, can develop violent behaviors as a way to cope with stressful situations."

"And then, when faced with a pandemic, you can see how many of them, in times of desperation, have turned to being aggressive toward others," said Espinola, who is also an assistant professor in the Department of Psychiatry and Behavioral Neuroscience at the University of Cincinnati College of Medicine.

The pandemic not only triggered the "fight" response in many Americans, but it also triggered our "flight" response to the added stress. More people left their jobs in April 2020 than any other month since the Great Depression (Iacurci, 2020). About four million people per month, 47.8 million, left their jobs in 2021, many by choice. Many don't want to return.

The pandemic has been especially hard on working women. According to the 2021 Women in the Workplace annual study by the consulting firm McKinsey & Company in partnership with LeanIn.Org, the largest study of women in corporate America, 42 percent of women reported burnout—up 10 percent from the previous year. WebMD defines burnout as "a form of exhaustion caused by constantly feeling swamped. It's a result of excessive and prolonged emotional, physical, and mental stress. In many cases, burnout is related to one's job. Burnout happens when you're overwhelmed, emotionally drained, and unable to keep up with life's incessant demands." (That was so me.)

Burnout isn't medically diagnosed, but it can lead to a physical and/or mental breakdown.

Some of the ripple effects of the pandemic were positive. It cleared away the stone to expose diamonds in the rough. Or gave us the extra push we needed to leave a job or relationship. It allowed us to slow down, spend time at home, and pursue old projects and new hobbies. We will never be the same. But maybe that's a good thing.

In his book *Life Is in the Transitions*, Bruce Feiler explained, "A lifequake is a forceful burst of change that leads to a period of upheaval, transition, and renewal." The pandemic for me, and many of us, was a lifequake. It turned my world upside down and broke me. But it also allowed for renewal, and time for me to rebuild into a more authentic me.

STOP SIGNS AND COVID-19

The World Health Organization reported in March 2022, two years after the start of the pandemic, COVID-19 led to a whopping 25 percent increase in depression and anxiety globally. Health workers were among the hardest hit, with exhaustion also triggering suicidal ideation. It also disproportionally impacted young people and women.

For me, the pandemic manifested itself as a giant stop sign, a boulder in my life path that halted me in my tracks. The wheels of my monkey mind spun into overdrive. So much so, I crashed in a daze. Thankfully, I'm emerging and moving forward as a better version of myself.

It also ushered in what has been coined as "The Great Awakening," where people suddenly realized the frailty of life and wanted to make big changes, especially in their jobs. This feeling brought about a significant shift in the workplace known as "The Great Resignation." I've experienced both, and then some.

The "Great Awakening" came when the pandemic brought a jolting wake-up call to our existing societal system. Other forces were at play to disrupt our comfort and success, for instance, the intensifying consequences of climate change and decades of systemic racism. Problems that previously were at a simmer came to a boiling point. The pandemic pushed us over the edge and shined a light on places and problems previously pushed under the rug or overlooked. We had copious amounts of time to reflect on what this meant for us as individuals and as a collective—more than any other moment in our lives—when the world came to a standstill, and we couldn't go anywhere. The pandemic also put extreme pressure on everyone to deal with the unknown on a daily basis. Some responded better than others. Rules changed constantly and not everyone agreed on the rules, leading to more chaos. We all had a new reality to deal with, whether we wanted to or not.

When COVID-19 was closing in on my city, my kids came home from school on a Monday in March 2020, and never went back for the rest of the year. We had to navigate the new reality of remote learning while my husband and I were figuring out remote working, zooming from meeting to meeting without even a bathroom or water break. They spent lots of time on their screens, for school or for fun, or they were sleeping. We had more family movie nights and dinners and made masks together. But everything was so unknown then—we didn't know how deadly the virus was, how it spread, how to prevent getting it. Anxiety in our household hit record levels.

As the pandemic was changing me and my family, it was altering the world around us too. The nonprofit public policy think tank, the Brookings Institution, warned at the start of the pandemic we would awaken to a new world when the crisis passed. The article admonished the individualistic "me-first" attitude of many of the first-world nations leading to a preventable large loss of life and livelihoods. We were rocked out of our complacency, as individuals and as nations, with the pandemic and the resulting "Great Awakening." The lessons we learned will be far-reaching, impacting us all over the long haul.

One aspect of our life that will never be the same again: work. We realized we can work remotely and be productive. Work from home wasn't a perk any longer. It was a necessity, and we were able to do it successfully, maybe even better than being in the office. We redefined what an "essential" worker was.

We took a harder look at women in the workforce, and their role as caretakers at home, and realized sometimes you can't be both. The myth of having it all or balancing work-life fell on its face as lines between work and home and school blurred. Many woke up to the true reality of work, and when and how and where it could be done, and which jobs were important. And what in life was important.

During (and in the wake of) the pandemic, millions of people switched jobs or quit the workforce altogether—many by choice. I was one of those. The pandemic, and the ripples from it, jolted me into the realization my approach to life wasn't working. I could control little, and I was stressed out by what I couldn't. I needed to make some serious adjustments to my outlook in order to still live. Trying to control everything clearly wasn't working. Doing what I always thought I "should" do led to a pit of despair. I knew I wanted something different, from what I did for a living to how I interacted with my family. I needed to resign from my old life and walk into a new one: A me who was more patient, present, and purposeful. One who listened to my whole self more and showed up in the world more authentically.

Only after a pandemic breakdown did I realize this.

The "Great Awakening" led to the "Great Resignation." People quit their jobs, or changed jobs, in record numbers since the pandemic started. During COVID-19, the US saw the greatest job loss since the Great Depression, with many opting out on their own.

That was only the beginning. Gallup's State of the Global Workplace: 2021 Report found 48 percent of the American workforce was actively looking to change jobs. (SHRM, 2022).

One could argue the Great Resignation was brewing well before the pandemic, and this Great Awakening pushed many workers over the edge to make a change.

In a 2018 Workplace Burnout survey by Deloitte, 77 percent of professionals surveyed said they had experienced burnout on their job, and 64 percent said they felt frequently stressed or frustrated. This was *before* the coronavirus.

"A lot of it comes down to how the pandemic has probably affected people's personal values and identity in some ways, kind of on a deeper level," said Kristen Jennings Black, an assistant professor at the University of Tennessee at Chattanooga who studies employee health and well-being. Then there's the massive shift to remote work. "Once we figured out we can work from home, many of us pretty effectively, it was just the question of, 'Well, why would I go back?'"

Less in-person time may have been good for productivity, our commute, and time available to do chores, but it wasn't good for our souls. In a March 2021 survey from Indeed found that 53 percent of remote workers clocked more hours each week than pre-pandemic, leading to even more feelings of burnout and reevaluation.

MELISSA'S STORY

Melissa, fifty-two, is an outgoing go-getter who has collected a few master's degrees, traveled, and had a fulfilling career. She never married or had kids—"not that I didn't want it, it just didn't work out that way," she said. Her life has been a series of events where she is in fight, flight, or freeze.

She said for the first twenty-four years of her life she was frozen. She said, "I was waiting to see what happened with my parents (who had an amicable divorce when she was nineteen), waiting for feedback, letting other people decide what I should do."

Melissa didn't want to deal, so she took flight. "It was my overcorrection of freezing," she said. She fled her hometown of Indianapolis after living there on her own for several years. She left to work and live in North Carolina, and then Washington, DC, only to return five years later. Her dad had survived a heart attack. It was a wake-up call for her, and she wanted to be closer to home and him. She started a clerical position at the university nearby and took advantage of the employee tuition break to earn her first master's degree.

She then went on to receive a second master's degree, followed by a two-hundred-hour yoga certification "to get her body back" after working full-time and going to grad school. It was 2019 and the future seemed bright. But not long after, the pandemic hit, and her mom suffered a stroke.

Melissa shared her story with me over a Zoom call. Looking much younger than a fifty-something, a vibrant soul with rosy skin, long highlighted hair, and thick, black-frame glasses, she talked to me from her home in Indianapolis. The oldest of three girls, she told me about her parents' divorce, her dad passing away from a second heart attack, and her two broken engagements.

A life of being frozen or fleeing all came to a head when the pandemic hit. "I wanted to take FMLA after my mom had the stroke, but my boss didn't understand. She discouraged it, but thought she was helping. I was so angry. I was angry about all of it. I was in fight mode. I was done freezing and fleeing," she said. So she took the anger that had been building for years and left her job of twenty-one years to strike out on her own.

"I think if I had taken FMLA, I maybe wouldn't have quit. But I was so exhausted I just couldn't have the conversation. To have to convince somebody and double ask them to sign the papers or who knows what, and it was all too much. I couldn't take one more thing. So I started figuring out what leaving would be like," she said.

Melissa decided to write a letter of resignation but realized she didn't know how to do one. So she googled "letter of resignation" and found a website with a form where a user could put in their information, "and it just spits out this perfect thing," she retold with an amazed tone in her voice. She said it was perfect and didn't burn any bridges.

"It was inspirational to have the letter generated for me. It wasn't emotional and I was so emotional! And then to just realize at that moment, I have never handled anything like that," she said.

And now?

She turned to art, freelancing, consulting, and living according to her own schedule. "Now it's fight, fight, fight. But also self-care. I'm out on my own, trying things on to see what might fit," she said. She has since created a business in IT, and contracts doing virtual events. She continues to serve others through teaching yoga classes.

Melissa is giving herself a chance to be perfectly imperfect and abandoning her cycle of freeze, flee, and fight. She is just being, even if it's hard.

Change makes us uneasy. Upheaval and transition tend to do that. But the promise of renewal is something we can all hold on to. It's what makes human beings resilient, especially in times like these.

THE NEW NORMAL

After Americans started to get vaccinated and the country was looking forward to being COVID-free in the summer of 2021, many people were feeling hopeful. In fact, Gallup classified 59.2 percent of Americans as "thriving" based on their responses to a June 2021 survey, the highest average score on that measure in thirteen years.

Then the highly contagious delta variant of COVID-19 happened. Harvard Business School social psychologist Amy Cuddy and writer Jill Ellyn Riley said what came next is what they call the "pandemic flux syndrome." It was a moment in time when we all came up for air when the pandemic seemed to be declining, only to suddenly bounce back with a vengeance. While it's not an official medical term, Cuddy and Riley described this syndrome as "blunted emotions, spikes in anxiety and depression, and a desire to drastically change something about their lives." At the same time we were feeling anxious about the virus, we were also optimistic about the future. These conflicting emotions are part of the "flux."

I strongly felt that desire for change and a more steady, centered life. After I returned from my FMLA break in April, I eventually left my job for good in June 2021. Like Melissa, I wasn't sure what was next. Leaving helped me continue on my path to healing. When I moved on, I felt like a weight had been lifted. I had exited a long, dark cave in a lifeboat and had made it out into the wide-open water outside. I was free. This freedom brought me a huge sense of relief, but it also brought more uncertainty.

As someone who likes to control things, the unknown can be hard. I not only worried about my financial future, but the world was also very uncertain—everything from the constant threat of the unknown with COVID-19 to looming disasters from climate change—hurricanes, wildfires, and floods—to social unrest with gun violence and the general "us vs. them" vibe of the nation. This constant threat from the unknown had me in flux for sure. I started to learn I wasn't alone.

Katy Milkman, a business professor at The Wharton School of the University of Pennsylvania and author of *How to Change,* said in her book that the ongoing pandemic hasn't allowed a lot of us to have a clean fresh start when we desired to have one. "Clearly demarcated fresh starts give us renewed motivation and help us pursue important goals. But for most of us, that clear fresh start hasn't materialized." I knew I wanted a new normal, but I didn't know what that was, especially given the unknown state of the world where everything was uncertain and upside down.

I liken it to a Band-Aid that is slowly being pulled off but never is quite removed.

Another factor is we are simply tired of the ongoing pandemic. As humans, we aren't designed for long-term trauma. In stressful situations, we rely on "surge capacity." As psychologist Ann Masten explained in an interview with science journalist Tara Haelle, "Surge capacity is a collection of adaptive systems—mental and physical—that humans draw on for short-term survival in acutely stressful situations." In other words, we are designed to survive an intense short-term stressor. All bets are off when it's an ongoing crisis or state of flux.

We are not meant to live in crisis mode for the long haul. Many who suffer from anxiety or depression like me feel like they are in a constant crisis mode. Now, with the pandemic, many have joined these anxious and depressed ranks, through no fault of their own. However, many were already there before the pandemic hit. The pandemic is what broke us.

THE PRODUCTIVITY MYTH

Part of the American dream is: if you work hard, you can achieve anything you put your mind to. I suppose that can be true for many people. I would argue we tend to hear about the ones who make it, rather than the ones who don't...so the myth perpetuates itself.

"American culture has popular theories about how to build a perfect life," writes Kate Bowler in her book *No Cure for Being Human (And Other Truths I Need to Hear)*. "You can have it all if you just learn how to conquer your limits. There is infinity lurking somewhere at the bottom of your inbox or in the stack of self-help books on the bedside table."

Bowler, who is living with incurable stage IV colon cancer and is a historian of Christianity at Duke's Divinity School, spent a lot of time in America's efficiency-obsessed "gospel of hustle," which always demands more, pushing us to conquer every to-do list (which would allow us to finally graduate to doing everything on our bucket list). In an interview with Clay Skipper for *GQ* magazine, she describes her book as a project in "trying to figure out what enoughness feels like."

"Self-help" books typically are all about how to be better, live your authentic life, be more productive, manage time better... just be "more." This adds to the pressure of hustle culture, rather than alleviating it. When are you enough as you are? What if we all worked harder at not working harder?

Bowler preaches about finding moments of "enoughness, without the promise of more." Is being slave to a to-do list a way to live your best life? I for one have had enough and am ready to experience enoughness.

Does work-life balance really exist? The ultimate goal for so many working women like myself is striking that balance—if we ever are able to do it. The aspiration was certainly a struggle before the pandemic. But with the added stresses from the pandemic—remote learning, childcare issues, health worries, and more—women are just plain opting out, and focusing more on the "life" part. A *Politico* article by Megan Cassella addresses this topic. She points out that in June 2021, 1.8 million fewer women were working than the previous year—57.5 percent of women aged twenty and older, the lowest number in thirty years (Cassella, 2021). She continues,

> *Economists caution that women's workforce partici-*
> *pation in the US has been stagnant for decades, more*
> *or less plateauing around 2000—a phenomenon*

experts say shows that even before the pandemic, working women needed more societal supports than were available. But the pandemic still dealt a resounding blow.

Is this also a blow to feminism? Look at how far women have come to get a college degree, fulfilling careers, and have a family and have time for herself, only to find out that it's impossible to "have it all." It's a myth! It's another long-simmering societal problem the pandemic made boil over. The reality is: women have been told we can do it all, but we don't get the support we need—from generous maternity leave policies, affordable childcare, and flexibility in the workplace. The pandemic has actually moved employers to offer more flexibility (out of necessity, first for the pandemic and now to keep the best talent), but we still have a way to go with maternity leave and childcare.

I've come to see work-life balance as more of a work-life flow. Balance insinuates equal, compartmentalized parts you shift around to make even. Flow is more fluid. It's when different areas of your life overlap, and some days it's more in one area than another. Unfortunately, it's taken my employers a long time to catch up and offer the flexibility I and my fellow working moms need and crave. Many women in the McKinsey study reported work flexibility would help them reach their career goals, and two-thirds said they want to work remotely at least three days a week post-pandemic (compared to 57 percent of men).

With the pandemic, companies are now starting to understand and accept this flow more—and see it can work. All of the companies who said you can't be trusted to work from home saw one of their top objections obliterated by the statistics that productivity increased during the pandemic. Now, as companies talk about returning to work, many employees are asking for hybrid or fully remote options so that they can take care of life and themselves. We all want flow, with more flexibility in hours and where we work, to ride the waves in the work-life ocean.

THE BOUNCE BACK

The pandemic has changed us. *The Lancet* commissioned a task force of psychologists to explore the mental health impact. They found that as a whole, we humans are more resilient than we give ourselves credit for being. This is true even after hard times, serious illness, war, and loss. We bounce back. The misery fades sooner than we think it will (The Lancet, 2022).

> *Study after study demonstrates that a majority of survivors either bounce back quickly or never show a substantial decline in mental health. Human beings possess what some researchers call a psychological immune system, a host of cognitive abilities that enable us to make the best of even the worst situation.*

> *Human beings are not passive victims of change but active stewards of our own well-being. This knowledge should empower us to make the disruptive changes our societies may require, even as we support the individuals and communities that have been hit hardest.*

This anxiety-ridden, work-life-flowing woman riding the waves of an unprecedented pandemic fell off her surfboard. But I got back up, and you can too. I needed to find a new normal, a way to be more resilient on the waves of life. The next section will illustrate how I bounced back from the depths and found my flow to live in "enoughness" every day despite what's going on in the world.

"Happiness as a byproduct of living our lives in a meaningful way is what we all aspire to, but happiness as the goal is a recipe for disaster," tweeted Lori Gottlieb, therapist and author of *Maybe You Should Talk to Someone*. My goal has become to find joy in the journey.

CHAPTER 3 QUESTIONS:

1. How did the pandemic impact your life? What changes have you made, if any? Which were by choice?

2. Did you experience a "Great Awakening" during the pandemic? How did you experience it in your life? Did you come to any new realizations? What are some of the implications in your life due to these realizations?

3. Were you part of the Great Resignation or do you know anyone who was? Why did you/they resign? Where are they now? Do you think you/they are now more aligned with your/their priorities and/or values? Why or why not?

4. Do you fight, flee, or freeze when you encounter a problem? Which do you do the most? Why?

5. What do you think of Kate Bowler's concept of "enoughness?" What does that look like for you?

6. Do you think there is such a thing as work-life balance? Why or why not? Do you have a hard line between work life and home life, or is it more of a flow?

7. Reread Lori Gottlieb's quote at the end of the chapter. What do you think she means? Is this true in your life? Why or why not?

PART TWO

LOOK

CHAPTER 4

Look Inward

———

"Your body hears everything your mind says."

— NAOMI JUDD

Not listening to your body can have dire consequences.

On my way back to me, I had to do some serious introspection. The fact of the matter is my body was screaming at me for months leading up to the January morning, and in some ways, for years leading up to that day, but I didn't listen.

Neha Sangwan, MD, specializes in internal medicine. She's the CEO and founder of Intuitive Intelligence, which educates about how communication impacts health and well-being. In her TEDx Talk, she shares that she has treated thousands of patients for heart attacks, pneumonia, and stroke. She strongly believes in the mind-body connection. Her work addresses the root cause of stress, miscommunication, and interpersonal conflict to heal chronic conditions such as headaches, insomnia, anxiety, and depression. Before she discharges her patients, she asks them a series of questions that include, "Why you?" "Why this (ailment)?" and "Why now in your life? Are there any messages you are getting from this?"

She explained that Brandon, fifty-two, answered, "I've always wanted to make my father proud. I have an Ivy League education, I'm married with two children, I'm a triathlete, and I've just sold my company for millions of dollars. And how come I just keep trying? The craziest part is my dad's been dead for five years, and I haven't slowed down." He continued, "This stroke came to tell me that I need to listen to my body. I'm exhausted."

I could relate to Brandon. He's about my age and extremely driven. Like him, the day in January told me I was exhausted. It was time to listen to my body.

I had to ask myself those same questions in my life. *Why me? Why this? Why now?*

THIRD TIME IS THE CHARM

The first time my body told me "enough" was in the summer of 2004. I had just turned thirty-three and was working full-time in downtown Chicago at a top ten international public relations agency. I worked long, intense hours. I was recently married and was going back to school to get my master's in marketing part-time at Northwestern University. I had a lot on my plate.

I vividly recall being on the L train on the way to work one day. It was hot outside, and hot and crowded in the subway car. We came to a sudden halt underground, as trains often do during the morning rush hour. The lights flickered on and off. The stop was still a few minutes down the tracks. I felt a flutter in my stomach that ran up to my heart and felt like it was going to crush my chest. I wanted to jump out of my skin and leap out of my seat, through the crowd, and exit the car I was in as soon as possible. But I knew it wasn't possible.

You're crazy! I screamed at myself. *Calm down!* I continued. *What is wrong with you? Pull it together,* the voice in my head admonished. All the while, my heart was beating rapidly and my breath was quickening. After what seemed forever, but in reality was probably only a minute or two, the train moved again and proceeded to my stop without further incident. But the damage had been done.

I was shaken, and shaking, as I walked to my building a few blocks from the train. Up the elevator I went to the fourteenth floor. The ride seemed especially claustrophobic to me that day. I grabbed some water before settling in at my cubicle. *What is going on?* I thought. *Something is not right. Am I having a heart attack?*

I continued to suffer shockwaves from what I felt on the train, with the walls feeling like they were closing in on me and my head slightly dizzy. I decided to call my doctor to make an appointment right away. We determined it wasn't a heart attack, but something new to me: a panic attack.

When I saw my doctor a few days later, she diagnosed me with generalized anxiety disorder, put me on some medication, and referred me to a psychiatrist. I didn't know it then, but my body was definitely screaming at me—something was going on that couldn't be fixed with a pill. Sure, the medication took away the panic attacks and dulled my anxiety. I didn't feel like I was going to jump out of my skin and flee the scene. I knew the darkness and fog were still there though. The medication released something in me that seemed to grasp my chest from the inside and put a lid on boiling water whenever the panic would start to rise from my core and make its way to my heart.

I felt slightly better, but I didn't get to the root of the problem or develop long-term coping mechanisms to prevent it from happening again. I soothed the hurt short-term. I did what thousands of Americans do each year when they suffer from anxiety or panic attacks: Take a pill. Talk to a professional. Put a temporary fix on it. This solution was Band-Aid that heals the wound but doesn't address the malignancy growing below.

A few months later, I learned I was pregnant with my first child. My husband and I were ecstatic. That meant I stopped taking my anti-anxiety meds but still was working with a psychiatrist. The excitement leading up to my twenty-week ultrasound in March 2005 was through the roof. I was finishing grad school soon and was thrilled to be a new mom soon.

But our excitement quickly turned to concern when the ultrasound technician needed to get a second opinion on some of the things she noticed during the scan. A doctor returned with her to tell us the words no parent ever wants to hear.

"Your daughter has some genetic anomalies that are incompatible with life," he told us gently. "We need to run more tests." So what started out as an innocent, happy occasion turned into a major lifequake, sending the towers of our parental hopes and dreams crushing to the Earth, with us facing a completely foreign landscape of genetic testing, trisomies, and the death—instead of birth—of a very wanted first child. We were devastated.

The panic I had worked hard to tame returned. I was utterly lost and broken. My baby girl, Faith Lily we named her, was stillborn on March 23, 2005. Genetic testing confirmed she had trisomy 13. She had parts missing from her heart and brain and other issues with her anatomy inside and out. But we got to meet her, and she was perfect to me. We were able to cradle her tiny, sixteen-ounce body in our arms, tell her we loved her, and stroke her blonde, peach fuzz hair, crooked pinkies (like her mom), and tiny toes.

We had a memorial service for her at our church, and I wept until I didn't have any more tears to cry. I took six weeks off from work. I had no energy and knew intuitively I needed to heal. This time I listened to my body. I paused life and took steps to take care of myself. I visited with friends and family. I took long walks with my husband at the local botanic garden. It was springtime and seeing the rebirth of the trees and flowers gave me strength and hope. I took Pilates with a trainer who helped me heal my post-pregnancy body. I started a journal of healing. I prayed and read books. I tried to center myself, return to a better me, and focus on what mattered, which to me was my relationships with myself and my loved ones. The panic I had struggled with took a vacation, along with my anxiety, as I rested my body, mind, and soul.

Life returned back to its regular cadence by the summer, but I had been changed by the chain of events of the previous year. I moved forward, eyes wide open, but still a little unsure about the future.

By August 2005 I was pregnant again and gave birth to a healthy girl in February 2006, followed by a healthy boy in August 2007. I had my hands full with two children under two. Slowly I lost my center again as I drifted into the vortex of motherhood and working full-time at an intense communications job. I had a miscarriage in the fall of 2009, but then a healthy child in November 2010. I still was on an extended vacation from any anxiety medication or additional professional therapy. Without them, few healthy coping mechanisms, and the pressures and emotions of work, life and loss, I started to feel the smoke monster creep back into my life.

My third child was three months old in March 2011. I was still on maternity leave when I was laid off in a corporate restructuring. I took the opportunity to get some more flexibility in my work life. I became a consultant and made my own hours. Except now I didn't have any boundaries between work and home, and I felt like I was working all of the time—in the little pockets of "free" time I had. I'd do all of my "mom" things during the day and then stay up until 2 or 3 a.m. doing all of the work I needed to get done for my clients.

In 2015, after a few years of keeping this schedule, the smoke monster reared its ugly head, eleven years after it first appeared in my life. The dread I felt that day on the L had returned in full force, this time stronger than before, literally knocking me to the ground when it visited me again one sunny fall afternoon, for seemingly no reason at all—other than my body said it had had enough.

I was having a bad day with nothing going my way and walked into my bedroom bathroom to collect myself. I felt the panic rise from my core and grasp my heart, but this time I had no medication to stop it, and no one was there to tell me I was okay. I collapsed to the floor and cried. I knew I wasn't right in my head…again. This time it was much worse. The monster had grown larger and stronger while it was lying in wait during those in-between years.

My husband had to come home from work and stay with me—I was afraid to be alone, fearful of what I might do to myself, or that I'd be too incapacitated to take care of our kids. I went back to the doctor, back on antidepressants, and back to a therapist—but this time, a new one. This time around, I knew what to expect with my pill/therapist routine. I didn't change much else, forgetting the lessons of healing from my time after Faith Lily, but remembering the Band-Aid fix the few months before I lost her when I had my first panic attack.

We are a nation of pill poppers. Have a headache? Take a pill. Feeling sad? Take a pill. *Medical News Today* said in a 2019 article, "Although some research links chemical imbalances in the brain to depression symptoms, scientists argue that this is not the whole picture."

We believe our mental health problems are the result of a chemical imbalance rather than an ailment of the soul. Or maybe we do know there's a deeper, underlying issue, but we don't want to do the work to stop the pain. This is also true for most ailments. We often opt for pharmaceuticals or surgery instead of modifying behavior. Taking medication is much easier, especially when you are a busy, working mom with three children. There is no time to stop.

According to the National Center for Health Statistics, during 2015–2018, 13.2 percent of adults aged eighteen and over overused antidepressant medications. Use was more than twice as high among women (17.7 percent) than men (8.4 percent). For women in their forties and fifties, like me, the number was even higher at 20 percent, or one in five women. Do that many women have chemical imbalances or is it something more?

Dr. James Gordon, a clinical professor in the Departments of Psychiatry and Family Medicine at Georgetown University, argues depression is not a disease, and that the related medications are overprescribed, in his book *Unstuck: Your Guide to the Seven-Stage Journey Out of Depression*. He writes, "It is a sign that our lives are out of balance, that we're stuck. It's a wake-up call and the start of a journey that can help us become whole and happy, a journey that can change and transform our lives."

Dr. Gordon believes the client taking an active role in the healing process is the key factor to successful treatment of depression without meds. Then any combination of complementary approaches like acupuncture, meditation and relaxation practices, sound nutrition, creative imagery, movement, and physical exercise can be effective.

I got to the point, after my relapse, where I was able to not need the antidepressants, but this time I kept speaking to my therapist. This was my lifeline that saved me when the smoke monster reappeared for the third time in my life, in January 2021. I knew from my previous two episodes my body was trying to tell me something. But this time was different—I was knocked down even harder than the first two times, so hard it almost killed me. My body definitely was trying to tell me something.

This time, I was really ready to listen. The third time was the charm.

THE MIND-BODY CONNECTION

So what was the difference this time? Maybe it was age. More likely it was my previous experiences with panic, and the very strong desire to never want the darkest depths again—especially since every time I was knocked down, the hit was harder. Hard enough this time to wake up!

I also became more aware of the mind-body connection. You see, I have been letting my mind rule my body most of my life. But my body has spoken to me in some very loud ways—and it has finally captured my attention.

What is the mind-body connection? According to Johns Hopkins Medicine, it is the belief that the causes, development, and outcomes of a physical illness are determined by the interaction of psychological, social, and biological factors. It is something in Western medical circles we are hearing much more about—but in Eastern medicine, the connection has been known for centuries. Western medicine is catching up though, with science and research to confirm and tell us why and how it works.

According to the National University of Health Sciences, Eastern medicine, also known as Oriental medicine or traditional Chinese medicine, is the oldest codified system of medicine in the world. It refers to a range of medical practices that originated throughout Asia, including acupuncture, Chinese herbal medicine, bodywork, tai chi, and qi gong. The basic philosophy of Eastern medicine practitioners is to treat the whole person, rather than the ailment, with a focus on prevention.

The Eastern philosophy of the mind-body connection is explored by Michael Singer in his book, *The Untethered Soul*. He explains, "you are not the voice in your mind, you are the one who hears it."

In my life, I've focused too much on what the voice was telling me instead of the person who was listening to it, reacting to it, and being deceived by it. Some people, especially those with anxiety, experience a "monkey mind"—where the voices in your mind are many and play tricks on you, like a troop of monkeys. Singer warns that a vast majority of what that voice says has no relevance on anything or anyone else but you, and that the voice talks because we are constantly trying to narrate our world to make ourselves feel like we have control. But as we know, control for a vast majority of what happens to us is an illusion. We cannot control external circumstances, as much as we try. But we *can* control our reactions.

He argues that if we instead tried to just consciously observe the world and not narrate it, in other words just *be*, we'd be more in tune with the person who watches the voice—what I would also call your authentic self. We need to look inward, get in touch with that observer, and move away from ignoring the observer or becoming obsessed with the voice in our heads, letting it rule us. We need to strike a balance between what the voice is saying and the person who is listening to the voice.

In his 2014 book, *The Body Keeps the Score*, psychiatrist Bessel van der Kolk, MD, who researches post-traumatic stress, notes that "neuroscience research shows the only way we can change the way we feel is by becoming aware of our inner experience and learning to befriend what is inside ourselves." He cites research by Joseph LeDoux that the only way we can consciously access the emotional brain is through self-awareness, also called interoception, Latin for "looking inside".

Healing our physical ailments means we have to deal with the voice inside our heads and acknowledge how our bodies are feeling. Harvard professor Elvin Semrad said the job of therapists is to help people "acknowledge, experience, and bear" the reality of life—with all its pleasures and heartbreaks. "The greatest sources of suffering are the lies we tell ourselves," he said. He believed people could never get better without knowing what they know and feeling what they feel. He said, "Healing depends only if you can acknowledge the reality of your body, in all of its visceral dimensions" (van der Kolk, 2014).

How do we look inside and start to get in touch with what our body is telling us? To tap into the observer and put aside the voice? Cognitive behavioral therapy has helped me. So has yoga (more on these later in the book). When I practice yoga, my teacher often asks me to "notice" and become aware of how I'm feeling: To notice sensations, my breath. Simply notice. It sounds so simple, but I've spent a good part of my life noticing everything else around me except how I'm feeling. I'm the queen of making myself so busy I don't have time to feel anything. But my body grew tired of being ignored and demanded to be heard. I needed to slow down and listen to my body. I dig in later with practical tips on how to establish a mind-body connection to bring about better health and build resilience. Just like Dr. Neha said, our bodies and minds are connected.

Another example she provided in her TEDx Talk was Juan, seventy-four. He said, "I don't think I ever remember crying in my life. Not when my children were born, not when my parents died. I look around in the world and I am dumbfounded by the connections people seem to have with one another. I've always felt isolated. This heart attack? Oh, I know what it came to tell me. It's the first time I've been able to express my emotions. I've cried for two days. I feel weak, Doc. Am I going to be okay?"

After that morning in January, I intuitively knew there was a better way forward, and I was ready for it. I was so broken, that the only way forward was to feel. To notice. To cry and feel uncomfortable emotions. Let the sadness flow through me instead of trying to control it. To connect my body and mind and find my authentic me in all its imperfect perfectness. I knew it was going to take more than a pill. I had to do the work this time. I was ready to try an integrated approach to healing and finding myself. I didn't want to go back to the old me. I wanted to shed my old self and my punishing ways. I yearned to be reborn.

CHAPTER 4 QUESTIONS:

1. Think about a past or present illness. Answer Dr. Neha's questions: Why you? Why the illness? Why then/now?

2. Have you ever experienced a panic attack? What happened? How did you treat it? What do you think brought it on? What changes to your life did you make after, if any?

3. How do you feel about pharmaceuticals to treat anxiety/ depression? Are you a proponent or opponent?

4. Do you think companies are doing enough to address mental health in the workplace? Why or why not? What can be done to reduce the stigma around mental health?

5. Have you ignored your body in the past and let your mind overrule it? When? What do you think it was trying to tell you? Did you listen? Why or why not?

CHAPTER 5

Look for the Helpers

"Look for the helpers. You will always find people who are helping."

— FRED ROGERS

We are all born into this life. But how many times are we reborn?

I knew my rebirth wasn't something I could do entirely by myself. Yes, I had to decide to move forward, and resolve to evolve…make a commitment to myself that I wanted something different. I now knew how important it was to listen to my body, and the consequences of not listening. But I wasn't sure where to go next.

As much as I wanted to, I knew I couldn't do it alone. I needed help from others. I needed to look outward and build a team.

As simple as asking for help sounds, this was not easy for me to do. I had spent most of my life doing things independently, going it alone—the Lone Ranger. It was the lesson I learned on my first day of kindergarten when I got lost: Don't rely on others. You have to rely on yourself. You are the only one who can't let you down.

BENEFITS OF HELPERS

To live our best lives and be our best selves, we need to learn to look beyond ourselves and ask for assistance. Here are a few reasons why you should:

- **It's an investment in *you* and your future.** In business, you have to spend money to make money. With the stock market, you have to invest to get a return. Same thing with help. You have to invest in yourself by getting help so that you can become a better you.
- **It allows you to take in the expertise and experiences of others where you may fall short.** I'm a communicator by trade. I'm not a finance person or a personal trainer or a nutritionist. Sure, I could try to get in shape or set a budget/invest by myself, but experts in the area can help me get there faster, and maybe better than I could by myself.
- **It helps you feel more connected and not alone.** Doing life and making yourself better with others is good for the soul. Remember, no man is an island. Research has found oxytocin, nicknamed "the love hormone," is released when we interact in positive relationships with others, increasing empathy, happiness, and life satisfaction.
- **It helps you put your problems in perspective.** I guarantee if you share one of your problems with someone else—whether personal or professional—you are likely not the only person to have gone through it, even though it may feel that way. Saying things out loud to another

person or people helps get it out of your head and not seem so big too.

- **It sets you on a better path than the alternative: burnout, anxiety, and depression.** Is it just me, or does the Lone Ranger ever seem happy? Batman? Any Marvel superhero? Being tough and not asking for help is not a path to happiness in my experience or others I've witnessed.
- **It sets a good example for others around you.** It's good for others, especially children, to see that you are not the Lone Ranger, that it's a myth, and that people can be successful and not kill themselves because they are doing it alone.

WHEN TO ASK FOR HELP

It takes more than hard work and a Puritan work ethic to be successful. But I didn't learn that truth until later in life. Hard work and sheer effort worked for me for a long time. Until it didn't.

After my failed escape attempt on the snowy January morning, I knew I needed help. A full-time, or even part-time, mental health program wasn't a fit for me at the time. So I decided to cobble together my own team to help me recover. I used body, mind, and spirit as my template. I started to explore experts in each of those areas.

Some of the people came to me because I was already connected to them, but I didn't have the time (or make the time) to reach out to them. Some of the people I found on Facebook or Instagram or YouTube—as life coaches and more were served up to me from the digital marketing algorithms that the universe had working in my favor.

The team I built included my primary care physician, a nurse practitioner who specializes in psychiatry, my therapist, a yoga teacher, a watercolor teacher, a life coach, a women's leader from my local church, and a few friends.

There were also online helpers, who didn't really interact with me personally but delivered the help I needed exactly when I needed it. These included people like Adriene Mishler of "Yoga with Adriene" on YouTube and a few other life coach gurus Facebook sent my way with the offer of listening to their free webinar (which usually ended with a pitch for their services). I listened to motivational speakers Tony Robbins and Dean Graziosi. I leaned in a little more to my friendships and my husband. This was my self-made "care" team that helped me climb out of the valley and on my path to wellness.

The phrase "it takes a village" usually refers to raising a child and is thought to have origins in Africa. The saying is true for me…it took a lot of different people in my proverbial village to grow me up and raise a new, better version of myself.

Sometime into my recovery, I was driving down the Kennedy Expressway in Chicago, in the vehicle I had used to make my escape. I was listening to a song—sung by Lin Manuel-Miranda, writer and producer of the Broadway hit *Hamilton*, and Ben Platt, the star of the Broadway show *Dear Evan Hansen*. It was a mash-up of the "The Story of Tonight" from *Hamilton* and "You'll be Found" from *Dear Evan Hansen*. The words from the powerful duo resonated with me and brought tears to my eyes as the morning sun rose behind the city skyline and warmed my face (and heart).

Step one: reach up and rise again. You will be found. Let the sun come shining in. The morning is breaking. All is new. You are not alone.

BOOKS & BOOK CLUBS

The self-help, or "self-improvement" industry was expected to be worth $11.3 billion in the US in 2021 and worth $14 billion by 2025, according to research company Marketdata. The company described this personal growth category as books, audiobooks, exercise equipment, weight loss services, live events, coaching, and seminars.

Since I had some time on my hands with my FMLA leave, I looked for some books that might help me.

Turns out, I had a lot to choose from. In 2019 alone, NPD reported sales of self-help books reached $18.6 million, experiencing a compound annual growth rate of 11 percent, showing no signs of slowing down anytime soon. Motivational and inspirational books, which are the most popular subject in the self-help category, accounted for sales of 4.3 million units in 2019, rising from just 1.4 million units in 2013. Books on creativity and journaling posted especially strong growth too.

Self-help books are sometimes good to read with a friend or two. I read the books that helped me with other trusted women—and we were able to explore and share the truths of each, and how they impacted our lives. It turns out the practice has been going on for nearly two hundred years in America.

Journalist Margaret Fuller started what is believed to be the precursor of modern-day book clubs. She held a reading circle, or what she called "conversations," in 1839. These women-only meetings in Boston were used to discuss books and the ideas they stirred in their souls.

Although exact numbers are hard to come by, the *New York Times* reports an estimated five million Americans belonged to a book club in 2014. The population of in-person book clubs skews heavily toward college-educated women, and a large proportion of these groups are single-sex, either by default or design. A 2014 survey by BookBrowse.com of American women who read at least one book a month found that 56 percent were in book clubs, and a majority of those were clubs that met in person.

Since the conversations of the 1800s to Oprah's and Reese's book clubs in the 2000s, the purpose of women gathering to discuss literature has spanned from consciousness-raising to self-help to individual improvement. "Book clubs provide opportunities for individual intellectual development, but they also emerge from a tradition that stresses the power of the group to implement social and personal change," says Pamela Burger, a writer, scholar, and educator, whose research focuses on gender and reading practices.

Christy Craig, PhD, a sociologist and researcher, found women turn to book clubs in times of uncertainty. They find solace in the books and in one another. The women she interviewed relied on their book clubs when they went through life transitions or hit stop signs.

"Women turned to book clubs to really construct important social networks, and that proved incredibly valuable," she said. She found through these book clubs, women found important partnerships to support themselves through difficult times, a sentiment that has proven true for me during the pandemic. I read books both alone and with friends to help me through the pandemic and my recovery.

What books will help you? This one is a start. Look at the bibliography in the back. Seek recommendations from trusted family and friends. Google it. Look at best sellers. Ask spiritual advisors. There isn't one answer—just take steps toward what interests you and be committed to moving forward.

CHAPTER 5 QUESTIONS:

1. Do you ask for help when you need it? Why or why not?

2. Which of the benefits of seeking help resonated with you most? Why?

3. Which books have helped you most in life?

4. Have you been in a book club or read a book with someone before? What are the benefits for you?

5. If you are not currently in a book club, would you want to be in one? Why or why not? How would you go about getting in one?

CHAPTER 6

Look to the Great Beyond

"Now faith is confidence in what we hope for and assurance about what we do not see."

— HEBREWS 11:1, NIV

When the world is upside down, what do you do?

When nothing makes sense anymore, what do you do?

When you, the people you know and love, the experts…when no one has the answers, what do you do?

You look beyond.

How do you define "beyond"? I call it that which we cannot see, the invisible. It's the spiritual realm. A lifeforce. An energy. As the award-winning female folk-guitar duo, the Indigo Girls would say, it's "the closer I am to fine." It's nature.

It's religion. Whether defined or undefined, organized or unorganized.

It's fueled by faith.

Mitch Albom, author of *Tuesdays with Morrie* and *The Five People You Meet in Heaven*, said in an Instagram interview (21:42) with former *Today Show* and *CBS Evening News* anchor Katie Couric when speaking about the loss of his adopted daughter, Chika, "faith is the thing that makes sense of all the bad things in the world. And the thing that you can turn to when things aren't going well."

The pandemic not only caused us to search inward and connect with others in new ways, but it also caused us to look beyond.

Lockdown, when the pandemic first began in early 2020, gave us a lot of time to think and reevaluate what was important. It gave us the opportunity to ask ourselves, what is this all for anyway? Most of us had the time, lots of time, to look inside and reflect. What does this mean? Why am I here? What's important anyway? When you strip away work, school, relationships, and activities. you are left alone. By yourself. Do I like the person I see? Am I making a difference? Am I where I want to be in life? What do I want to do with my time here?

I suppose we all come to a point in our life when we ask these questions, but there are a few times in my life when I think society collectively had that time for introspection. The pandemic was the biggest event of my lifetime—and it was for most people alive during this time, I'd venture to say.

When the answers are beyond us and we face a collective foe like the pandemic, many of us tap into our spiritual selves. The side that doesn't have a scientific explanation—the part of us that is unexplained and relies on faith and intuition, God, the universe.

Many of us like to believe something out there greater than us exists, greater than this Earth. How can you look at the stars, planets, and the Milky Way and not think something bigger than us out is out there? That we are just a speck in the universe and our time is a blink of an eye in history?

To move forward, I knew I had to come to terms with my spiritual self. To be okay with it. To know, and accept, that faith and a belief in something bigger was okay. Even more than okay—necessary to move on. That I am part of a collective and it's my role to figure out my place in that. To shine as brightly as I can, as we only get one shot at it.

In *Think Like a Monk*, Jay Shetty, a former Hindu monk, shares how your spiritual life is the way you consciously do ordinary things. This is where ritual comes into play and can help you grow spiritually. It's when you do things with intention that you feel centered and can grow.

Sometimes I enjoy doing the dishes or laundry and get lost in the ordinary task. It helps me stay present. Finding joy in the simple things. Being present and noticing the world around you—focusing on the task at hand.

Another book that exemplifies this for Christians is *The Practice of the Presence of God* by Brother Lawrence. A humble friar who lived in France in the seventeenth century, he spent much of his days working in the kitchen. A classic still today, more than three centuries later, Brother Lawrence provides simple steps to connect with God daily. He found joy and God's presence no matter where he was or what he was doing.

Around Christmastime, in 2020 I bought a little wooden desk decoration for a gift exchange game. It said, "Find Joy in the Journey." I didn't really understand what it meant at the time, but I liked the saying and thought it would be good for a friend who liked to hike and was part of the game. As luck would have it, I was the person who ended up with it in our grab bag game. Having it perched on my dresser this past year, it has come to take on new meaning as the words in a fancy script were burned in my brain each day. It reminds me to live with intention, so I can find joy in the journey.

It can start with meditation, where you slow down, pause, and sharpen your senses. You notice your breath, sensations inside your body or on your skin, sounds you hear, aromas you smell. You may think of meditation as being in a quiet place of solitude sitting cross-legged, but it can also be in a classroom, office meeting, outside on the street, or in a forest on a hike. It's more of a state of mind than a place.

I always wondered why Buddhist monks would create elaborate designs from colored sand called mandalas—even spend days, weeks, or years on it—only to destroy it in the end. Maybe you've done a puzzle, spent hours or days toiling on it, only to pull it apart and put it back in the box. The sand mandala is a meditation that is supposed to show the impermanence of life. It's also the process that brings you "closer to fine"—not the end goal itself.

I think this is why many people are not happy in their careers. The "goal" of a paycheck isn't enough sometimes (and can be easily taken away). They still may be unhappy, even if they have a good-paying job in a good career. If you are not enjoying the simple things, the process of doing your job, loving what you do, then it doesn't matter about the other things you get from it. Satisfaction ultimately comes from believing in the value of what you do.

I couldn't be satisfied at my workplace if they didn't value my contributions, so I had to find another route to achieving worthwhile goals. Receiving a paycheck wasn't enough for me.

Jay Shetty advises, "To live intentionally, step back from external goals and look within." I'd argue you also have to look outside yourself too.

IDENTIFY SOMETHING OUTSIDE YOURSELF

As I mentioned before, I profess to be a Christian. I believe in God and the Holy Trinity. I believe in Jesus and that He died for my sins. I believe I will go to heaven when I die. I pray to God to help me through hard times and to help and comfort others. I try to please Him and not man. This is what I believe. It helps direct my life. It is greater than who I am. I am hopeful for other people to find God, or something that is bigger than them that they can connect to and find hope and faith in. Something that makes them a better person, and the world a better place.

Also, through my yoga practice, I have come to a better understanding of my body-mind connection, energy, and life force. Through yoga, I can still my mind and be present, simply noticing how my physical body is feeling and the world around me. I strive to do things that put me in this present state. It can be as simple as pausing and taking a breath wherever you are. It can be a meditation practice.

It can be a hobby that helps keep you in the moment, whether it be an artistic pursuit like painting or sewing, a sport like running or tennis, or something like birdwatching or playing chess. Whatever "it" is, find something you enjoy doing that keeps you in the moment, where you can lose yourself and all sense of time and place. That's when you can calm your mind and connect with your spiritual side—the energy that is bigger than yourself.

For me, I love to create and find peace in the process. While I'm no artist, I find great joy in watercolor painting and the creative experience. I lose myself. It's the same with gardening and taking photos.

Adele, the multiplatinum, multiple major award-winning singer, told talk show personality Oprah during an interview about her album, 30, that she loses herself when she sings. It's like an energy outside of herself takes over and she's able to sing and perform extremely painful and personal songs that somehow seem to touch millions around the world and tap into human emotions that transcend time and space.

To me, that's what being spiritual is all about—tapping into an energy that is part of all of us in a way that is personal to you. That energy is bigger than me, bigger than you, and it's part of the universe. Sometimes it delivers things to me, like people and opportunities. It could be God, the universe, or coincidence. I tend to think it's more God and/or the universe.

TAP INTO YOUR SPIRITUAL SIDE

To tap into both of these spiritual sides of me I do a few things. For my life as a Christian, I go to church, pray, read the bible, and listen to a Christian radio station (positive, encouraging K-LOVE). I have relationships with other Christians that encourage and challenge me "as iron sharpens iron" (Proverbs 27:17, NIV).

My stepmother, Colette, seventy-six, said she depends heavily on God to get her through hard times. She and my father, who she has been married to since 1979, have a strong faith. She's been the primary caretaker for my dad, who was diagnosed with a rare brain disorder, multiple system atrophy (MSA), in 2014. It's a fatal disease with no cure that slowly shuts down the body's automatic systems, like digestion, circulation, and breathing.

My father has also lived with bipolar disorder, and we suspect he also has Lewy body dementia. He gets around with a walker and hasn't driven since his MSA diagnosis. He repeats himself sometimes, forgets common words, and sees and hears things no one else can. Lately, he's lost his appetite and is losing a lot of weight. All of these overlapping conditions, the anxiety, and sleepless nights for both of them make care-taking difficult. How does she do it?

"I rely on God to get me through the unknown. Honestly, I trust in Him the most. I know He will never leave me. My faith is the strongest it's ever been," she said. As we consider caregiving decisions moving forward, it can be overwhelming. But Colette finds solace and comfort in her faith. She does this through prayer and reading her Bible daily.

The Bible teaches that we consist of body, soul, and spirit: "May your whole spirit, soul and body be kept blameless at the coming of our Lord Jesus" (I Thessalonians 5:23, NIV). By being wholly filled with God in every part of our being, God can be expressed through us.

Our physical bodies are something we can see and touch. Our spirit and soul are invisible to the naked eye. We commune with God through our spirits. It is at the center of who we are. Our souls hold our spirits. We can experience God by exercising our spirit, for instance, when we sing worship songs, pray, or read the Bible. These practices can fill us with God's spirit, allow him to work through us, and center us.

Me, I also get centered through yoga by practicing daily. This can include breathing techniques (pranayama), physical poses (asana), and/or meditation. I try to be aware of what my body is telling me and focus on being present as much as possible—and not focus too much on the past or worry about the future.

Like Colette, I also rely on God, and what I call universal energy, to move me through tough spots. This keeps me on my journey when it gets too tough to go it alone. When I think I can't go on., I tap into the spiritual realm—something I can't see or touch, but can feel moving inside and around me comforting me. I can feel it through the love and interaction with others—that is beyond my explanation. It's the "coincidences" in life you can't explain.

Sociologist, life coach, and author Martha Beck notes, "Psychiatrist Carl Jung had a term for meaningful coincidences: *synchronicity*. He wasn't just talking about interesting surprises, like getting a lottery number that matches your birth date. Synchronicity is what happens when seemingly unrelated events coincide in improbable ways that have some sort of significance for you. Jung believed synchronicities were evidence of a unifying consciousness at play in the universe, creating physical manifestations of what's happening in our psyche. We can use these synchronicities to better understand ourselves.

"I do think that something more than chance is at work in the universe. While reality usually babbles in the meaningless music of randomness, it sometimes speaks to us in a language we understand. Why? Maybe because our small consciousness is intimately bound up with consciousness writ large, and we may need a little nod from a force that's greater and wiser than we are."

She invites us to consider the possibility that we could be connected to everything in the universe, everything in the universe could be connected to you, and meaning flows between the two in a mysterious constant stream.

One summer night, I was sitting outside with a friend in her seventies enjoying the mild weather and sipping on sangria from Costco.

She's gracefully aged by keeping her mind and body active. She shared with me some of her spiritual beliefs, which one could argue helps keep her young at heart.

She believes in a universal intelligence. Raised a Christian, she believes this intelligence is God, a gender-neutral God, but it can be whatever you want to call it. She said we are all part of it. "It's not positive or negative. It's neutral. It's an energy that's kind of out there floating around. You need to learn how to tap into it." She said it could be through yoga, meditation, or by being intentional about acknowledging it in some way, like with prayer. The key is to calm yourself, get centered. Be neutral.

This is a very positive, healing source for me. It helps calm my fears because I know I am surrounded. It's all around. It's like we're swimming in this vast ocean of wonderful affirmative intelligence, or energy. And why shouldn't I participate in that?

She said she is intentional about counting her blessings each night. "I'm always very grateful. I have to put myself in a positive mindset. I can't sit and replay bad scenarios and then ruminate about bad things."

She also intentionally asks the universe for help with her problems. "If I have a particular problem, I say, 'This is my problem. Could you please put in my path the information I need that will help me resolve this problem in a positive manner?'" She said she always gets an answer.

Is her life always "happy" or perfect? Far from it.

In terms of evolution, we are hardwired to learn more from unhappy experiences. That's what has helped us survive as a species. Fear. 'Don't touch the fire. You'll burn yourself.' That's hardwired in the limbic system of our brain. I've opened myself up to the fact that hard things can be positive things. We learn from them.

All that said, I believe the spiritual forces moving around us are not always good, or even neutral. I believe there is negative energy in the universe, and also the opposite of God (the Devil). Chinese philosophy teaches the concept of yin and yang, a fundamental principle that guides the universe. Yin is characterized as negative, passive, and feminine, among other things, whereas yang is seen as positive, active, and masculine, among other things (APA Dictionary, 2022).

The negative forces work against us and try to bring us down. There is a fight for our soul. We can learn from the negative without succumbing to it. This is why I try to be mindful and tap into the positive energy of the universe and of God.

DEMYSTIFY YOUR DHARMA

Building on the concept we are all connected to a bigger universal energy or lifeforce, some people talk about "doing your dharma," a spiritual concept linking our destiny to the collective, not the individual. Ancient yogic texts describe dharma as inner wisdom or cosmic guidance that governs not only you and me as individuals but the entire universe (Shaissha, 2022).

In *Think Like a Monk*, Shetty wrote about finding your dharma, or purpose, which is your passion in the service of others. He said response from others when you use your dharma should be positive, and that going against it can make you feel out of control and exhausted. How do you find your dharma?

To get started, Shetty recommended a Vedic personality test. I took it, and my top result was the Leader profile.

According to Shetty, "Leaders" are natural leaders and he used words like courage, strength, determination, focus, and dedicated to describe them, also noting they are led by "higher morals and values." I found the description to be accurate—in my senior year of high school, I was voted "Most Dedicated" by my classmates. On a more serious note, I have always gravitated toward the role of a leader in my personal and professional life, for better or for worse.

Shetty warned, "Going against your dharma makes you feel out of control and exhausted." I found this to also be true. When I was trapped in a job that only wanted me to do the status quo, to not lead, be innovative or have any new ideas—and I was to only implement others' ideas, with no input or creativity of my own—it was soul-crushing.

Sahara Rose, called a "leading voice of the millennial generation" by Deepak Chopra, host of the number one spirituality podcast on iTunes, *Highest Self,* and best-selling author of *Discover Your Dharma: A Vedic Guide to Finding Your Purpose* also helps people identify and build a dharma blueprint. Her online quiz helps you discover your Ayurvedic mind-body type.

Derived from the Sanskrit words, "ayur," or life, and "veda," which means science or knowledge, this natural system of medicine came from India more than three thousand years ago. Ayurveda teaches that there are three *doshas* of energy in our bodies related to nature that circulate and govern our physical, mental, and emotional well-being. Everyone has all three, as well as their own unique balance of each. The idea is to know which one you are and then strive to keep all three in balance through nutrition, exercise, and stress reduction. It's a holistic approach to health with a focus on preventative care (Johns Hopkins Medicine, 2022).

Rose's dharma quiz revealed my primary archetype was an entrepreneur with the dosha being pitta, which is closely related to fire and water. After reviewing the archetypes, I thought they were helpful and provided some good insights on my archetype was at its best, in addition to some things to watch out for.

My takeaway from my shallow dive into identifying my dharma is: Knowing your life purpose can help steer you in life and connect you to something bigger than yourself. If you get off course, or off-center, you take steps to bring yourself back on course. This is especially helpful to build resilience when you get knocked down.

The same holds true when you are happy and/or successful. You shouldn't get too carried away or off track, as that can lead you off center. The idea isn't necessarily getting to one particular goal or accomplishment—it's really about maintaining a process, or journey and staying aligned and healthy so you can accomplish your purpose for the greater good. Service to others can help you feel grounded.

I like how Ayurveda attempts to explain universal energy and the energy that flows within us, and how to keep it in a "flow" state—not too much, or too little. It's like riding a wave and constantly checking in with yourself.

EMBODIMENT: CONNECT YOUR BODY-MIND-SPIRIT

Embodiment explores the relationship between our physical being and our energy—it's how our body, thoughts, and actions interact. When we experience events, they can impact our physical, emotional, cognitive, and spiritual being as a whole.

We should use our senses, not just our minds, to process and feel events and our emotions. We can get to the embodied state through practices like yoga, dance or movement therapy, visualization, sensory awareness, and progressive muscle relaxation. It could also be mindful eating or taking a cold shower or jumping in an icy lake in the middle of winter (Madeson, 2021).

All of these examples get you to feel and process things in your body instead of ignoring your body and what it feels and tells you a lot of time: 'I have to go to the bathroom,' 'I want to sleep,' 'I'm hungry.'

With these exercises, we actively listen to our physical bodies through our senses. What do you hear? Smell? See? Taste? What sensations do you feel on your skin? We then process emotions and feelings and tap into energy by quieting our minds and letting our bodies lead the way.

Research has shown that practicing embodiment techniques has been effective in treating depression, anxiety, and eating disorders.

Melissa Madeson, PhD, LPC, an adjunct professor, yoga therapist, and author writes,

> *Essentially, any movement or focus on physical sensation can become an embodiment exercise. The key is to do the activity mindfully and notice your senses (smell, sight, touch, taste, sound). Things like taking a bubble bath, baking/cooking, and gardening can become healing tools for clients if they engage their senses, do things slowly, and allow themselves to connect more fully to their body and the specific experience.*

We can mindfully do anything, even ordinary tasks like washing the dishes. Angela Mitchell, a working mom of a tween and teen, finds washing the dishes each night grounds her. She puts on some music, early '90s rock like Blind Melon or Mother Love Bone, and loads the dishwasher or may even throw in a load of laundry. She does this ritual almost every night around midnight. Why? She explains, "It makes me feel accomplished, more prepared for the next day. I have a hard time falling asleep unless I do it."

Another way to practice embodiment is to try walking a labyrinth. These are also called meditation circles and can be found on the grounds of parks, hospitals, houses of worship, or formal gardens. They are pathways, usually circular, that lead to a center. It's different than a maze because you won't get lost. They can be painted on the ground or created with shrubs. The point is to walk it with an intention, to help you feel calm. It's not about the destination—it's about the journey. When you get to the center, you should feel more relaxed.

A labyrinth is an ancient tool of meditation for humans. "They're found on Greek pottery, Spanish petroglyphs or rock carvings, and in walkable form, on the floors of medieval cathedrals in Europe," according to WebMD. Research has found walking labyrinths helps reduce your blood pressure and slow your breathing.

Tapping into my spiritual side and universal energy and practicing embodiment has helped me feel more grounded and centered in a world of the unknown and chaos. It's helped me process my environment and made me calmer, less anxious. It's been a life-giving way for me to develop resilience and move on past the "hard things." It's allowed me to blossom into a lotus flower and be reborn.

A SOUL STUDY

To do some "soul repair" during my recovery, I did a deeper dive into yoga, with the help of my local yoga studio which offered a "Soul Study and Yoga Immersion." The sixteen-week session taught me more about the practice, how to be embodied, and the mind-body connection. Kelli Wefenstette, thirty-seven, was my instructor. She has a five-hundred-hour yoga certification, with two hundred hours in Hatha and three hundred in elemental yoga.

The "Soul Study and Yoga Immersion" training is designed for people who want to go deeper into their own practice. The soul study for me was a safe space to learn what yoga is, what it has been, and what it could be to me in my daily life. It was also a place for me to do some soul healing after what I'd been through and learn how to make myself whole. If I couldn't run away to a convent or a retreat, to me, this was the next best thing.

I reached out to Kelli a year after I finished the training. She shared the big picture of what we accomplished in our training in an interview in June 2022. She started with the basics. "Yoga is the pathway to meet one's true self," she said.

"It's not a coincidence that yoga also corresponds to things we know in psychology and spirituality and sexuality, physiology."

Kelli teaches the koshic model of yoga, where the body has five layers that surround the soul. They are like nesting dolls, where the outer, largest, slowest, and most tangible layer is the physical body. Then there's the energetic body and the mental body, intellectual, and spiritual.

Kelli led her students, like me, to learn about the eight limbs of yoga, along with the five koshas. She taught us about elemental yoga, which considers the balance of space, air, earth, fire, and water in our bodies. She believes these teachings are not in competition with one another, and in fact, there is a lot of overlap. She hadn't encountered a place where they taught a full integration or balance of these different approaches—the closest was in Ayurvedic practice.

In Kelli's class, I learned how to recognize my own imbalance. I examined the different layers of myself and how they were communicating to me. This included everything from being tired to headaches to digestion, to my emotions. I just had to figure out where and what was my body communicating.

We learned this throughout the program, especially during asana practice, where she always invited us to "notice." Just notice. Ever hear that in a yoga class? It means to listen. Listen to what your body is saying to you. What is it saying?

I learned to tune into my body when I wasn't on the yoga mat too. When I was tired, I noticed. When I was feeling anxious with a racing mind, I noticed. Then I learned to adjust. For instance, I might give up my to-do list and go to bed instead of plowing ahead, telling myself I don't need sleep. Or when I feel my monkey mind spinning like a hamster wheel, I notice.

This usually happens late at night in bed or when I first wake up. I stop and place one hand on my heart and one on my belly and I practice box breathing. This is when you breathe in for four counts, hold for four, breathe out for four, and hold for four. Then you start over. It calms your nervous system.

Kelli taught me to notice and identify the kosha where it originated. She taught me about tools—many based on centuries-old practices like breathing, also known as pranayama—I had at my disposal to help. I learned how to balance my elements.

The mind is represented by air. I definitely have an overactive air element. I learned how to balance that with grounding "earth" poses, yoga poses on the ground. Every yoga pose is associated with an element.

An especially healing earth pose for me is savasana or corpse pose, where you lay on your back on the ground, totally relaxed. It feels so good for me, and lots of others who are go-go-going all the time. Being still during the rest time associated with it can be hard, though. It relaxes your nervous system, your mind, your heart, and your breathing, and reduces stress. It can aid headaches, fatigue, and anxiety. It is a blissful, resting pose for me.

The thing about what works for us in yoga (and in life) is that it is always changing. It's adaptable and meets us where we are. But we are creatures of habit and routine. Sometimes changing that routine is hard, but it is also necessary to get out of our comfort zone, to bring ourselves back into balance for long-term health. Moving back into balance sometimes means we have to go through pain to get there.

I feel better equipped to face what life throws my way because of the tools Kelli has taught me. But it all starts with just noticing and listening to our bodies. I've learned to evaluate myself and know when and how to use these tools. We have the power and capacity to bring ourselves back to balance. It's always a work in practice though—a lifelong journey.

Kelli told me, "There's no part of us missing. We just need to redistribute misalignment and redistribute energy. There might be too much energy in one part, and it's stuck from getting to another part, but it's up to us to just redistribute it. And it's a constant balance, right? It's not like how you are today will be how you are tomorrow. That's why we practice."

"We're not static beings. We're constantly moving and flowing and changing and that's actually a sign that things are working," she said.

CHAPTER 6 QUESTIONS:

1. What does spirituality mean to you? How do you tap into your spiritual side?

2. How can you strengthen your spiritual side?

3. What is your dharma? How does that impact your relationships? Your career? Your priorities?

4. What do you do to feel embodied? What techniques can you try to add to your current routine to help you feel more embodied? What new activities can you try to experience embodiment?

5. What are the benefits of yoga? How can you start and/or deepen your practice?

PART THREE

LISTEN & LET GO

CHAPTER 7

Listen to Your Authentic Self

—

"Honesty and transparency make you vulnerable. Be honest and transparent anyway."

— MOTHER TERESA

Suddenly, I'm awake. It's 3:45 a.m. according to the alarm clock by my bed. I can barely make out the fuzzy numbers without my glasses at this ungodly hour. My room is dark except for the flashing white star Christmas lights in my bedroom window. I groan and turn toward my husband. "What day is it?" I think to myself. "Tuesday." Oh yeah. The shocking events from the day before come flooding back to my head.

"You're a failure," the voice tells me. "You should be ashamed of yourself," it continues. "Why did you tell that story? You talk too much. You need to listen more. No wonder why that happened. You are such an imposter. You didn't deserve that position anyway. It was only a matter of time before they found out." My body is tense, my eyes close tightly. I feel my heart ache and a wave of sadness and shame come over me. My head is pounding. I want to crawl out of my skin and hide. But I'm already in bed. I turn over again.

"I'm okay. Everything is okay. God loves me. I'm okay. Everything is okay. God loves me," I keep repeating in my mind, hoping to crowd out the bitter words of self-hate and disgust. "Everyone makes mistakes. You are resilient. This doesn't define you." I continue on with this conversation, going back and forth, thinking about my future and what's next and desperately trying to fall back asleep.

I breathe. Breathe in. Breathe out. Take a few conscious breaths. Place one hand on my heart and one on my belly. Two hours pass before I finally drift off again.

THE VOICE VS. THE OBSERVER

As Singer writes in *The Untethered Soul,* we are observers, the ones who listen to the voice in our heads. *We are not the voice in our heads.* The more we can get in touch with the observer, the closer we get to our authentic selves. But how do we get there?

Singer argues we need to quiet that voice we hear and try not to narrate our present and just "be." We should try not to dwell on the past or worry about tomorrow (hello, racing thoughts at night). This is easier said than done. The truth is it's a practice, something we need to strive for every day. Some days are easier than others.

BECOMING AUTHENTIC

"The privilege of a lifetime is to become who you truly are," said Carl Jung, the famous Swiss psychiatrist and psycho-analyst. He is talking about becoming your authentic self, who you are as a person, outside of any external factors that may define you.

For me, this means I'm not my job. My career—my successes and my failures—do not define me. My authentic self is not my husband's wife or my children's mother. My authentic self lies outside of these identities.

To be authentic may sometimes lead to you standing out from the crowd. For example, when US gymnast Simone Biles, who arguably is the greatest female gymnast of all time, dropped out of the Tokyo Olympic Summer Games in 2021 because of mental health issues, she was called a quitter and many other things. But she knew her authentic self enough to know her health was more important than any medal. She was able to sacrifice her chance at breaking world records and winning the most gold medals ever, things she had practiced countless hours to achieve and sacrificed so much time and hardship to do. She gave it all up to be true to herself.

Many people believe being your authentic self is to follow your passion—but as Biles shows, it's more than that. We can't do things only to please others.

Despite the stress, Biles said, her time at the Tokyo Games helped her realize that her self-worth was more than how other people saw her. She said her worst moment was "proba-bly realizing or recognizing that I would only be remembered for my medals." Thankfully, she was able to overcome those fears.

"One morning I woke up and I was like, 'I'm more than my medals and gymnastics, I'm a human being,'" she said. "And I've done some courageous things outside of this sport as well, and I'm not a quitter and it took all of that realizing to see that, because…if this situation didn't happen I don't think I would have ever seen it that way, I would have never been able to walk away and think I'm more than just gymnastics and medals."

BE PATIENT

I'm an impulsive and impatient person sometimes. This natural inclination likely fuels my anxiety and drives me further from the person I aim to be. I needed to find something to slow me down, help me reflect, and help me be more me. The "Yoga Immersion and Soul Study" I completed was online because of COVID-19, even though it was through my local yoga studio. The purpose was to align "your true self with your dharma to experience complete balance within yourself, relationships, and the world." *Whoa, that's deep, right?* I signed up knowing I needed to do some reflection and exploration about myself, to get unstuck, and get to a place where I was more "me."

I embarked on a journey to acknowledge my strengths and weaknesses, accept myself where I was at without judgment, and have compassion while just being and noticing why I was feeling or acting the way I was. If I did all that, I could take steps to get more centered. I learned a lot of those tools in my training.

After the course, one of my classmates made us all bracelets as an act of seva, or service, with our intentional words. I had two, "patient" and "present." I needed to be patient with myself, and others, in order to be present. I also needed to remind myself to be present and not worry about things in the future. I needed to remember to not let my anxiety get the best of me.

Yoga is one tool I use to help me slow down and get back to myself. Other tools I picked up or sharpened in class include journaling, meditation, breathing, and walks in nature. These things all help me be more patient and present. Now when you read this list, you might roll your eyes or think, "I've heard that a million times," or "I've tried those things, but they don't work for me," or "those aren't for me."

I'd just say that I'd bet at least one would work for you if not all. I encourage you to explore. Dig deeper into the ones you have dabbled in or others you already engage with and try new ones you haven't tried. Be open to yes instead of saying no. You might get closer to your authentic self—the one who listens to the voice—along the way.

JOURNAL

It is important to take time out to reflect on who you think you really are. Growing into your authentic self, or working to uncover that person, can help us navigate the ups and downs of life with a stronger sense of self-worth and confidence. One way to do this is through journaling.

Karianne used journaling as a device to get her energy flowing again and discover the next step in her path after losing her job. While processing this difficult event, she said she journaled every day for two years—sometimes twice a day. She now aims for once a day. "I would listen to myself through journaling. I was open to 'going there.' It allowed me to get out the stuff going on the inside through stream of consciousness writing," she said.

Journaling helped her learn who she was, and it was okay to have different emotions. "I needed to spend time feeling, but corporate America tells you to leave it at the door."

A longtime friend, Roddy Chong, is a successful motivational corporate speaker and a lead violinist for the arena rock band Trans-Siberian Orchestra. He's one of the most disciplined, goal-oriented people I know. He told me about journaling, "There's got to be hundreds of thousands of articles about how this helps the brain and the body...whether it's getting out ruminating negative thoughts onto paper or writing out your goals."

He likes to track his day, rating on a one to five scale each hour how he's feeling overall in the "basics" (i.e., mood, energy level, motivation level, focus). He also lists his larger goals. He prefers handwriting vs. typing it or putting it in his phone because he doesn't want to get distracted by email or social media. He looks for patterns in his rating system, to see how successful he is in achieving his goals, and adjusts as necessary.

Roddy sometimes looks back on his notebooks for patterns and insights. Once he finishes a notebook, it goes in a plastic bin that he stores in a closet in his tiny bachelor pad in LA. He said he has several bins full of journals, but he never looks at them. Why? "I just use them to monitor my day, be present. I don't really need them later."

Another form of journaling is called Morning Pages. First coined by Julia Cameron in the book *The Artist's Way: A Spiritual Path to Higher Creativity*, this exercise is meant to be done by hand, first thing in the morning, in a notebook of your choice. The goal is to empty your mind and clear the way to get the creative juices flowing.

You are supposed to write for fifteen minutes anything that comes to mind, from to-do lists to thoughts about what to cook for dinner and then whatever more formed thoughts come. This type of stream-of-consciousness writing peels back the layers of the onion to get to the *aha* nuggets of insight. It can be a warm-up for whatever is next in your day or a way to clear space to make room for new, fresh thoughts and ideas. It can also bring you closer to your authentic self, as you clear the voice(s) out of your head and get to just *being*.

In *Writing Down the Bones*, Natalie Goldberg said that through writing, "some part of us can walk through the humming mosquitos and touch a very clear part inside us. We can ignore the negativity and constant chatter of the inner critic." When you write, "you disappear: you are simply recording the thoughts that are streaming through you." This is a process that helped Karianne.

Goldberg advised when sitting down to write something, "Don't hold too tight; allow it to come out how it needs to rather than trying to control it" and "take chances. You will succeed if you are fearless of failure."

The reward? "The writing process is a constant source of life and vitality," she said. It's also something where you can release pain and suffering. "Writing is deeper than therapy. You write through your pain, and even your suffering must be written out and let go of."

My go-to when life is extra hard is journaling. I have a journal of healing for when I lost Faith Lily that chronicles my journey through the valley of death. I have a COVID-19 journal. I started it a month before lockdown and continued it all the way through to the vaccine. I have yet another for my recovery after January 2021. It helps me get out of my head, but it also helps me process and reflect on difficult emotions after traumatic events, and watch the aftershocks reverberate throughout the pages.

I would argue we are our most authentic selves when we journal. Goldberg uses it to "make myself strong and come home, and it may be the only real home I'll ever have."

Goldberg rereads her writing notebooks.

When I reread my notebooks, it never fails to remind me that I have a life, that I felt and thought and saw. It is very reaffirming because sometimes writing seems useless and a waste of time. Suddenly you are sitting in your chair fascinated by your own mundane life. That's the great value of art—making the ordinary extraordinary. We awaken ourselves to the life we are living.

In our interview, Melissa shared how journaling regularly was too routine for her; instead, she does a morning gratitude check.

I've tried journals. I'm not very disciplined in doing them. But I'm also completely aware of how I feel most moments. When I wake up in the morning, usually pretty early, I may or may not feel stress in my forehead. "Is it a relaxed forehead, or do I have 'the pinch' with thoughts running?" I ask myself. "Why is my forehead already pinched? Why did I wake up like this?" And I know, I just need to relax. So I think of what I am grateful for and it immediately sets my day in a better direction. So cliche, but I swear it works.

Melissa is a strong believer that our bodies tell us when it's time to stop and let go. Or a life circumstance will. She advises that when it happens, "Lean into the full stop. Don't just see a stop sign and roll through it. Really stop. Sleep a lot. Get healthy. Get calm. Try not to be triggered. I needed to not be triggered. It's a very triggering world right now. Fight for your peace."

DEVELOP A MEDITATION PRACTICE

Another path to getting in touch with your authentic self and remaining present and centered is to meditate.

According to the research-based health and wellness website *The Good Body*, it is estimated that between 250 million people worldwide meditate, with 14 percent of the US population reporting to have tried it and more women than men practicing. In 2019, the top ten selling meditation apps generated $195 million in sales. Two of the most popular are Calm, which was the top downloaded meditation app in 2021, and Headspace, which reports thirty million users in 190 countries (Buccholz, 2021).

A 2016 research study showed 76 percent of those surveyed used meditation for general wellness. Other reasons included relief from depression, anxiety, and stress, and to improve energy and focus.

Other studies have shown regularly meditating can reduce the risk of diseases like Alzheimer's, improve productivity at work (one study said by 120 percent!), and reduce school suspensions.

Meditation also helps clear your mind, to stop the monkey mind and get in touch with the one who observes the voice. If you suffer from an anxious and overactive brain, meditation can help focus you to start your day but can also help reduce stress and anxiety to calm your mind so you can fall and stay asleep at night. Maggie Ryan, an assistant editor at *POPSUGAR Fitness* and *Yahoo! News* contributor, tried ten-minute sleep meditations from the Headspace app for a month and now has no trouble falling fast asleep.

I use meditation via the Calm app. I don't do it as often as I should, but every time I do I'm glad I did. I feel calmer and more centered each time. I only do it for ten minutes, so it is not a huge time commitment. The trouble for me is finding a quiet space in my home to do it uninterrupted. I keep track of how I feel before and after I meditate through the app. I did it more often during my recovery. Now, I try to do it sprinkled throughout my day. I pause and notice where I am and try to tune into my senses. It slows me down and centers me.

Sometimes when I pray, I also feel like I am meditating. I'm focusing on God and having a conversation. I'm saying what I'm thankful for and also asking for help with issues in my life, or others. I tend to ask for strength a lot, especially when I feel like I'm in the valleys. Similar to meditation, prayer can center you and calm you.

GET IN TOUCH WITH YOUR SENSES: SINGING BOWLS

Viewing her on my computer screen, sitting cross-legged in front of four large crystal singing bowls, Karianne looks like a modern Nordic princess who is serious about her craft. She gently eases calming tones out of them with two hollow, plastic mallets. The bowls are of the same height but have varying colors and diameters. They're made of pure quartz and sand, in a process that heats the mixture to about four thousand degrees. They also are infused with gemstones and minerals, one of the reasons they are even more powerful.

While the scientific evidence is not clear, a wealth of anecdotal evidence indicates singing bowl tones have positive physical, mental, and emotional effects on those who hear them. One observational study examined the effects of singing bowl meditation and found after twenty minutes it significantly reduced tension, anger, fatigue, and depressed mood among the sixty-two adult participants. Metal bowls have been used throughout history for food and Buddhist religious offerings. In the 1960s, both metal and crystal bowls started being referred to as singing bowls, gaining popularity in anxiety-laden Western nations for use in sound therapy practices, meditation, and yoga classes.

Gently touching the bowls with the tamper and slowly running each stick along the outer edges of the crystal elicits a vibrating deep sound that summons the stars and energy in the universe. It causes my brain to tingle behind my ears on the side of my skull. The tones are strangely soothing and seem to resonate in the center of my chest.

As I watch Karianne's performance and practice, it seems to come from a renewed soul that has traveled life's valleys. It's from one reborn from years of small steps on a journey toward being her true self, gathering new tools, and relying on old ones along the way.

GET IN TOUCH WITH YOUR SENSES: AROMATHERAPY

I love the smell of freshly baked chocolate chip cookies, ground French roast coffee brewing in the morning, the dewy air, and plants breathing after a rainstorm in a deciduous forest. All of these aromas center me, calm me, return me to me, and help me be present. When I practice yoga or write, I'll sometimes burn a scented candle to designate it as a sacred time for myself. Many of the candles are gifts or purchases from favorite travels and places. The ritual of the lighting and the steady scent also calms my brain.

When it comes to essential oils from plants, science is starting to confirm the therapeutic benefits. According to the Mayo Clinic, some research has found the use of essential oils can provide proven health and wellness boosters such as relief from anxiety and depression, improved quality of life for people—especially those with chronic health conditions—and improved sleep.

For me, I use essential oil mixes on my pulse points to help center and calm my mind when feeling stressed and sometimes spray my pillow with lavender before bed. These scents tickle my brain and make me feel calm. I like to keep essential oil rollers or sticks at my desk, as well as calming sprays, to give me a pick-me-up and mindful break throughout my day. It's a little time-out where I take time to pause and breathe.

The growing market for aromatherapy diffusers, at $1.59 billion in 2019 with a projection of reaching $3.22 billion in sales worldwide by 2027, also says something about their use and efficacy. They are most popular in North America, especially for residential and spa use. I use one in my bedroom at home, especially in the winter, to help me think of other seasons and nature. Speaking of which…

GET IN TOUCH WITH YOUR SENSES: NATURE

Probably the best therapeutic remedy for me where I use all of my senses is nature. The sights, sounds, smells, and feel of nature soothe my soul. I especially love the beach. The pebbly sand on my feet, the salty air, the rhythmic crashing of waves, and the warm sun on my face heal me like nothing else. Walking in a garden, stroking pine needles on a tree, or taking in the vibrance of velvet roses stirs something in me that is otherworldly. When I hurt, I go to nature. When I need to think, I go to nature. When I need to decompress, I go to nature.

Laura, fifty, a mom of three adult children and one of my best friends from high school, explores the great outdoors to process her stressful job as a social worker and the issues she faces in life. She's an avid hiker who loves the mountains. "The wonder of being in the wild gives me the space that my thinking self, my feeling self, and the deepest part of my soul need to put all the challenges life brings in perspective. I gain so much insight on the trail," she told me.

The world tends to demand much but being out in the wild where I can wander allows me to stay curious about life instead of rigid; it keeps me open to possibilities, and by being connected to the natural rhythms and beauty around me I am more aligned with my greater purpose.

Hiking is so much more to me than just a hobby or an activity. Nature is more to me than something pretty to photograph. I know I'm not alone in feeling that way. Years ago, when I completed a pilgrimage on the Camino in Spain there is a greeting one pil-grim says to another, "Buen Camino," which trans-lates to "good way." Pilgrims know each person is on their own journey. It's a way of acknowledging each other by saying, "I see you. Enjoy your journey." And knowing their path is different than mine. It's power-ful. You are a part of something. Connected. Seen. I had wondered as I walked what it could be like if we all greeted each other this way on our life journeys.

Science is behind the benefits of nature too. In his book, *Last Child in the Woods: Saving Our Children From Nature-Deficit Disorder,* Richard Louv writes that a widening circle of researchers believes the disconnection from nature has enor-mous implications for human health and development. The quality of exposure to nature can affect our health at almost a cellular level He talks about "ecopsychology" and nature therapy, which touts the benefits of what the earth does for our physical and mental health.

Chinese Taoists created gardens beneficial for health over two thousand years ago, and in 1699 *The English Gardener* advised there is no better way to preserve health than spend-ing time gardening or walking in a garden. That sentiment grew in America, with therapeutic gardens becoming pop-ular in the late 1700s onward. Dr. Benjamin Rush, a mental health pioneer and signer of the Declaration of Independ-ence, wrote, "digging in the soil has a curative effect on the mentally ill."

Louv's book shares many studies that show how even looking at nature through windows can improve physical health for people vs. those who don't have those views and also protects against stress. He makes the case that some mental ailments that are treated with medication, such as anxiety, depression, and attention disorders, could benefit from "the use of nature as an alternative, additional, or preventative therapy."

Our senses are what make us human. There are many other tools I don't mention here that can calm you and center you through your senses. What moves us is unique to each of us. Celebrate your humanness by taking time to enjoy what gives you life, helps you be present, and brings you to your authentic you.

CHAPTER 7 QUESTIONS:

1. As children we are our most authentic selves. We are creative, imaginative, and impulsive. We do what makes us truly happy and we express freely how we are feeling. Think back to when you were a kid—what did you want to be when you grew up?

2. What does balance look like for you? How do you know you're not in balance? How do you bring yourself back to center?

3. Have you tried journaling? Why or why not? How was it helpful? If not, what are some steps you can do to try?

4. What is your perception of meditation? How do you think it could benefit your life?

5. How do you use your senses to calm yourself and destress? Write a list. Try to do one of those things every day.

6. If nature were a prescription or pill, how could you incorporate it into your life daily? Weekly? Monthly? Write yourself a prescription.

CHAPTER 8

Listen to Your People

————

"Healing is an act of communion."

— BELL HOOKS

According to the English rock band the Beatles and their song "With a Little Help from My Friends" on their 1967 album, *Sgt. Pepper's Lonely Hearts Club Band*, we can all get by with the help of our people.

The hardest parts of life are made more bearable if we have people to share it with or walk alongside us—people who value the real you, who really get you, who are kindred spirits, and who can remind you of who you are. Your tribe.

Having a tribe can help you reconnect with your authentic self when life throws you lemons. Even though you may want to stay in bed and pull the covers over your head, connecting with a member of your own tribe can provide balm on your battered soul and help remind you of who you are and what's important in life.

Strong friendships are good for your health. A 2017 research study suggests if you have strong friendships, you'll probably find it easier to handle the inevitable ups and downs of life. They are also good for preventing loneliness, reducing stress, providing emotional support, helping with personal development, and creating a sense of belonging and support through life's challenges.

But that sense of belonging is eroding for many. In *The Atlantic*, Derek Thompson wrote, "Before the pandemic, the office served for many as the last physical community left, especially as church attendance and association membership declined. But now, even our office relationships are being dispersed."

To his point, thirty-five million Americans live alone today according to the US Census Bureau, which is 28 percent of all households. In 2018, long before the pandemic lockdowns and the launch of the work-from-home experiment had begun, a study by the Kaiser Family Foundation showed that one-in-four adults already felt lonely or socially isolated all of the time.

Jon Levy, author of the *New York Times* best seller *You're Invited: The Art and Science of Cultivating Influence,* wrote, "The greatest punishment we give people in society is either solitary confinement or banishment from the group. It's because we're not meant to be isolated and—without connection to others—we suffer psychologically and emotionally."

Companions don't even need to be real to offer support. A pilot study led in 2021 by my friend Professor Valerie Jones at the University of Nebraska-Lincoln found that personal voice assistants (PVAs), like Amazon Echo, statistically reduced the participants' loneliness. Conversing throughout the day with a PVA helped the senior citizens, seventy-five and older, who lived alone feel less lonely, especially those who had reported the highest scores of loneliness before the study.

Research by Brigham Young University professor Julianne Holt-Lunstad shows the most important predictor of living a long life is social integration, meaning how many people we connect with every day. A study from the University of Chicago confirms this by showing it's the routine interactions we have with myriad people in our day-to-day interactions that sustain us. According to Holt-Lunstad, the impact of lacking social connection is equal to the risk of smoking fifteen cigarettes a day—greater than the risks of obesity, excessive alcohol consumption, and lack of exercise.

"Quite simply, human relationship is as essential to physical, psychological and emotional well-being as food and water," said US Surgeon General Vivek Murthy in *Together: The Healing Power of Human Connection in a Sometimes Lonely World*. Face-to-face meetings, in-person collaboration, and "micro-moments" of community at work are what give people the essential feeling of belonging.

People need people, people! It's what makes us unique and human.

LISTENING TO YOUR FRIENDS

Friends can be placed in different categories. Close friends are those you can laugh with or cry with and be with unconditionally. They love you no matter what and will tell you if something is in your teeth when you are talking to them. This is the family you choose. Consider yourself lucky if you have at least one such person in your life. (If you don't I have a few ideas to help. Keep reading.)

I am extremely thankful to have these friends in my life. I have friends from high school I've known for more than thirty-five years. Some I see a few times a year, others I speak to weekly. I know I can pick up the phone and ask them for anything and they'd be there. They help keep me centered and real. We've supported each other through moves across the world, job loss, death, milestone birthdays, kid troubles, marriage troubles, nervous breakdowns, and more. We've made sense of the political and societal upheaval in the face of an unprecedented virus.

These are the friends who had my back when I was at the lowest of lows. They helped remind me of my worth, of better days, that hard feelings are temporary and do not define me or the rest of my life.

Another group of friends gets together about once a month. We share a meal, laugh, and just hang out. We come as we are—each from different walks of life—and accept each other for who we are and forgive imperfections. Conversation and laughter are easy. I don't have to think about anything, I just am. They also helped put things in perspective when I was at my lowest, reminding me I was more than any one moment or job, that I had value, and they were there to walk alongside me.

Another friend I've known since we were twenty-somethings, at the beginning of our careers, living life like we were on the TV show *Friends*. We've helped each other through boyfriends, husbands, kids, our crazy job industry, and more. She has also been a rock for me during this time.

Other friends who pass in and out of my life have offered support, advice, and encouragement. Friends from childhood, high school, college, grad school, work, church, yoga, parents of my kids' friends, and neighbors—they are part of my team.

Karianne relies on her team to help her get closer to her authentic self. When it comes to getting support for the dreams you dream, she said, "Own it, tell people what your dream is. I cannot believe the power of sharing out loud what you want to make happen. You confess, and they invest. And they remind you, pulling you toward that goal."

Friends can definitely pull you along to help you achieve your dreams. Take writing this book. I've wanted to give up so many times. Different people encouraged me, but it was my close friends who were the most convincing. They reminded me why I was doing it—for myself and to help one other person.

One friend explained I suffered from what author and researcher Brené Brown called a "vulnerability hangover." It's when you feel naked, ashamed, and scared after sharing your story. You regret it. You feel like you've shared too much. The same stories that allow you to step into courage and empowerment, and promote positive conversations that could lead to change, can be equally devastating for the storyteller.

For other goals, like losing weight, reading a book, or running a marathon, having accountability partners can help. I joined a weight-loss community to hold me accountable (thanks Noom) and lost thirty pounds. I know I'll finish a book if I'm reading it with friends. I was able to train for and complete a marathon with running partners. Having others hold you accountable to meet a goal makes you more likely to achieve it. In fact, you have a 65 percent chance of completing a goal if you commit to someone you will do it, and a *95 percent chance* of success if you have a specific accountability appointment with a person you've committed (Newland, 2018).

Research also shows that people can help other people through tough times even when they aren't close friends.

Psychiatrist Dr. Dennis Charney, co-author of *Resilience: The Science of Mastering Life's Greatest Challenges*, calls it having a "tap code," after the technique used by the Vietnam POWs to survive mentally and emotionally being locked in solitary cells.

By tapping a special secret code on the walls of their cells, prisoners communicated with each other despite being in individual cells.

"If they didn't have the ability to communicate with the person who was in solitary in the next cell, it would have been extremely difficult to psychologically survive," Charney said. "So we make the point that everybody needs a tap code, everybody needs that kind of support during tough times."

MOLLY'S STORY

Molly Monroy, thirty-seven, left a job with one of the largest tech companies in the world after burning out during the pandemic. She was in the same lifeboat as a few of her close friends.

With a wholesome, girl-next-door look and earnestness about her, Molly has always been a high achiever, excelling in high school and college. She told me when I interviewed her in 2021 that she fell into tech public relations after attending the University of North Carolina at Chapel Hill and eventually found herself at Microsoft.

But despite all of her achievements doing what she calls "meaningful, but lucrative work," she said she felt a little lost, depressed, and in a brain fog during her last eighteen months in her tech PR job. This time happened to coincide exactly with a global pandemic, getting remarried, becoming a stepmom, and moving across the country. Her body was trying to tell her something wasn't right even though outwardly, everything looked perfect by the world's standards.

> I am someone who's always been independent, who's put career first. I kept seeing these red flags that I needed to change my focus. Instead, I saw them as challenges to be overcome rather than to stop and actually pay attention to them. Suddenly, I was just

breaking. One of the key lessons is to pay attention to the stop signs if something is there and floating around in the back of your mind. It's there for a reason. Don't push through, don't ignore it.

I'm the oldest child. I was raised by parents who pushed me very, very hard. I had to go to the best school I could get into. There was something in my mind telling me I needed to work for the best PR agency, I had to work for the best tech company. But I don't—there was no true reason. It's not something I wanted. It's just what I was always conditioned to believe, it was what I was supposed to be doing. When I finally stopped and said, "You know what, I don't have to do this anymore. I can change. It's okay." And kind of forgiving myself for being that way and realizing that it wasn't actually me.

She is finding a lot of people in her circle of friends are going through a similar life transition. Two of her closest managers and mentors went through the exact same life circumstances—divorce, then remarriage. Leaving the same company she worked at and redefining themselves. Their shared experiences and support helped her find her new normal.

She added, "I also have a close friend in Boulder who was going through the exact same thing as I was. She worked for another big tech company and left, maybe two weeks before I did. Also, my sister who's much younger than me just moved to Colorado and is going through a lot of life change. Just a year or so behind me. So I feel like I have support from friends and family, and definitely my husband."

FINDING FRIENDS

Some people feel like they may need a little extra help to find friends. Maybe you moved to a new town, are in a different life stage than your other friends, have lost touch with your old friends, or all of the above. Some people in this situation are enlisting friendship coaches to help them create a game plan to find and keep friends (Glantz, 2020). This can include holding you accountable for the ideas you discuss together and following up to encourage you and ensure you act.

For those who want to try a more conventional way, friendship takes two things: intention and investment. Be intentional about spending time with people you want to get to know or care about as a friend. Invest in them and put in the time and effort. Once you water the plant of friendship, it will likely blossom. If you are putting in the investment and being your authentic self and it doesn't work, or you are treated poorly time and again, or they are not honest and trustworthy, it may be time to move on.

Grace, fifty-two, is part of a group of five females she calls the "apocalypse moms," she told me when I spoke with her in June 2022. The women, who had children in the same classroom at school, came together during the lockdown. They would keep in touch via group text and still use it today. Each person plays a different role in the group. One is a scientist, seeking the facts in everything, another is the emotional one, concerned about everyone's feelings, and another is the organizer. When one of the moms was diagnosed with stage 4 cancer, they all played a part in her care, right down to the meal trains organized by Grace, and the online fundraiser, organized by another.

"COVID made people more real, more authentic, more purposeful," she said about her social interactions since the pandemic. But it's more than about the relationship. "People crave connection. You can be in a relationship and be lonely."

She admits it's hard to make friends at this stage in life. "I gave up a lot of myself for my kids," Grace said, sharing that she and her husband would soon be empty nesters. "I am looking to fill my time more purposefully. I like being with people, I want connection." She is intentional about meeting new people through friends of friends. Some of it is to network for business, but she's also looking for people who have similar interests and things in common, beyond their kids going to the same school.

Most of us develop friends from shared experiences: growing up in the same neighborhood, going to the same school or house of worship, playing on the same team, and working at the same job. As you age, those opportunities are fewer, and you have less time to invest in "free time." Outside of work and home obligations, there's not much time for yourself, let alone friends.

Julie Beck, a writer for *The Atlantic* and creator of its series "The Friendship Files," interviewed one hundred sets of friends over three years. She found six common themes that help form friendships and maintain them:

ACCUMULATION

The more time you spend with a person, the closer they become. This makes sense as some of my closest friendships were formed at school or work. Obviously, you need to spend time with any relationship to make it grow.

ATTENTION

A connection can come at any time, or any place—you just have to be open to it. "Because as much as we may feel like our social networks are set and settled, it's never too late to meet someone who will be important to you for the rest of your life," Beck writes. This can even happen in midlife. Talk to the people in your yoga class or at the gym. I've stayed friends with people I've met on airplane flights. I've met other parents at my kids' activities by taking time to interact with them and not stare at my smartphone. The trick is to be present. If you click with someone, take the next step.

INTENTION

Beck advises that friendships may require a type of courtship or intentional pursuit to get going. "It takes energy and thought, and our mental and physical resources are often spread thin. In other words, friendships take work."

RITUAL

Traditions can fuel friendship. One group of friends and I try to get together once a month for a meal, and if it's around a holiday, some crafting. I've belonged to book clubs and church small groups. Some people play a sport together regularly or watch the Super Bowl together each year. Some take annual girls' or boys' trips.

I've been a Girl Scout troop leader for several years. We do the same ceremonial opening and closing at our meetings. We recite the pledge and Girl Scout Promise at the beginning. At the end, we gather in the friendship circle and hold hands (right arm over left). We think of one thing we are grateful about for the person next to us, or a wish we have for them, and then squeeze their hand. Once the wishes silently and solemnly (if no one giggles) work their way around the circle, we sing "Make New Friends." I hope the ritual of the ceremony stays in their minds, and the message in their hearts, long after the meeting is over.

IMAGINATION
Friends sometimes show they care for one another by doing radical acts of kindness, outside what is typically expected from a friendship. Being a surrogate for your friend's baby. Going to therapy together. Buying a house together. Sending an anonymous gift card when they need it. Dropping off flowers at their house for no reason.

GRACE
"I've come to believe that friendship doesn't always have to be about presence; it can also be about love that can weather absence," Beck writes. I agree. The best friends are the ones you can pick right up with where you left off, and just enjoy each other's company. Friends need to be forgiving and give each other grace. I know mine have with me, and I afford

the same forgiveness to them. We are all imperfectly perfect, after all.

FINDING A LIFE COACH

As you build and rely on your tribe, consider enlisting a life coach, especially if you are going through a challenging time or life transition. They can help you get unstuck and see new perspectives. Just like an athlete going through a rough spot or who wants to improve, your life coach is trained to provide you with the outside perspective you might need to achieve your goals. They are a great accountability partner.

Molly said, "I've been an athlete my whole life, a distance runner. So the mind-body connection has always been really important. I always have listened to my mind and thought pain was something to be pushed through." Leaving the corporate world has allowed her to slow down and sit with her thoughts. With the help of a life coach, Molly's finding a path back to her true self. Her life coach is "very good at asking questions and getting me to think about things I don't want to think about and how I'm feeling about certain things. She is definitely the voice reminding me to slow down and be curious." Her coach is helping her overcome the guilt she has for leaving Microsoft and taking time for herself—and helping her understand she isn't a failure, that it's a progression, a bold move, what she needs to do for herself, and that's okay.

Molly said, "She sees things like when I just start talking that I don't—that's like, oh, wait, let's pause on that. Then we spend twenty minutes on it. Like, wow, that was a really insightful thing that was in my subconscious that I would have never picked up on."

"The biggest thing she's encouraging me to do, she actually said, 'find your inner child.' Because I was complaining about my stepson, taking three hours to walk from his school three blocks to the car, because there's a blade of grass that he has to stare at for ten minutes and it was driving me insane. She told me I should be more like that. Tap into your inner curiosity. If a random thought flickers to your mind, grasp onto it. So I am, and I'm really starting to feel the brain fog lift and the energy come back because of that."

Life coaching is part of the $2.85 billion global industry of professional coaches that includes executive, career, leadership, and even nutrition coaching. The International Coaching Federation (ICF) estimates there are seventy-one thousand professional coaches worldwide and twenty-three thousand based in North America.

How do you find a life coach? The ICF, the largest governing body of the life coaching industry, provides credentialing for coaches. Look for ACC, PCC, or MCC credentials next to their name. You can also ask friends for a referral. Prices can range from $50 to $500 a session and up. You can also buy packages. You can select one on your particular issue. Is it a career transition? Midlife crisis? Challenge at home or work? A life coach exists for everyone.

Life coaches help you achieve personal and professional goals, help you become "unstuck" in situations, and help you be your best you. They aren't therapists, but they help you see the bigger picture of where you are, and where you want to be and create a plan to get you there. The ICF defines coaching as "partnering with clients in a thought-provoking and creative process that inspires them to maximize their personal and professional potential."

My life coach, who I found through a LinkedIn recommendation, specializes in career transitions and growth for senior leaders. She was in my field (marketing and communications) before she became a coach. So she really understands the dynamics of my career and career path.

She has provided valuable insight into my "why" and helped me reframe a lot of my life and career experiences so I can process my hurt, get through to who I'd like to be, and ensure I present myself in a way I'd like to be perceived. We've done assessments and reviewed results and implications on what makes me tick, what gives me energy, and what is likely to trip me up. She's the one who introduced me to the idea of writing this book and encouraged me along the way when I wanted to throw in the towel.

I've discovered through my work with her that my greatest strength is my greatest weakness. I'm honest, but to a fault sometimes. My downfall has been not being always able to "read the room," and sharing more "truth" than is needed, or appropriate, for the moment. She's helping me see there is a time and place for everything in order to "win" the game of work.

As someone who was a high performer in school, I've learned it's a different set of rules and expectations in the working world, which has led to some huge bumps and bruises along the way. The hardest worker, smartest worker, or even the most productive worker (hello productivity myth) does not always win the day. However, the savviest one does. It's been a hard lesson to learn.

FINDING A THERAPIST

When you suffer from anxiety and/or depression, like me, getting professional help is a good idea. To explore the physical ramifications of my 2021 depression, which included not being able to get out of bed, losing interest in everything around me—including my hygiene and my family, feeling a crushing sensation in my chest, even though I had no history of heart problems, and trouble falling asleep along with waking up in the middle of the night, I visited with my primary care physician.

She thought my physical symptoms were being caused by my brain and referred me to a psychiatrist for additional help and to get the right mix of medications. Unfortunately, the number of psychiatrists available and the number of people who need them are far apart. I left voicemails for two before finally connecting with one at a clinic—and the only one with availability was a nurse practitioner who specialized in psychiatry. She was understanding and a great help.

This all happened during the pandemic. So I get the mental health system was overwhelmed. But it was that way before the pandemic too. Stacy Weiner of the Association of American Medical Colleges reported the United States was suffering from a dramatic shortage of psychiatrists and other mental health providers in 2018, with the shortfall particularly dire in rural and urban areas.

The fact of the matter is that good mental health help is hard to find.

If you are looking for a one-stop shop, talk therapy provided by someone who can prescribe medication, then go the medical doctor route (psychiatrist). But, as previously noted, finding one is time-consuming and hard. They can also be expensive depending on the insurance you have. I'm someone who has good health insurance (but lives in an urban area), and I had a hard time. What about the twenty-eight million people in the United States who don't have insurance?

If taking medication is not something you desire, or even if it is, I'd highly recommend enlisting the help of a licensed therapist for talk therapy. The key word here is "licensed." Then you know they will have a certain amount of training and schooling to get the license from a governmental or organizational body and are professionally equipped to guide you to the next best version of yourself. My therapist is a licensed clinical social worker.

Licensed therapists are also in short supply these days. But the good news is telehealth has made them much more accessible. This is one of the silver linings of the pandemic.

When everything was going virtual—school, work—medical visits went virtual too. For the first time, private insurers and the Centers for Medicare and Medicaid Service (CMS) relaxed in-person visit rules and said they'd approve telehealth payment on a national level for things like mental health visits, opening the doors to treatment where they were closed previously.

The pandemic has also brought about increased awareness of the importance of mental health, and insurance companies are now more likely than ever to cover some or all of the cost of the visit. Many employers offer employee assistance plans too.

If you can't find a therapist and need help right away, as of July 2022, you can call the national mental health talk line if you are having a mental health crisis: 988.

Prior to the pandemic, I found my therapist through an app called Talkspace. Talkspace is an online text and video chat therapy platform that offers access to therapists who cover a broad range of mental health issues. It was a low-barrier way for me to access a mental health provider. I took a quiz and the app provided three options for counselors. I picked mine because she specialized in cognitive behavioral therapy (CBT). Since our thoughts drive our behaviors, this type of therapy aims to introduce patients to new techniques to reframe our thoughts. If you change your thoughts, you can change your behaviors.

A huge part of overcoming anxiety and depression is getting help with reframing what's in your mind and moving away from self-destructive behaviors and beliefs. My therapist helps me repair, build, and navigate relationship issues, and examine past issues and traumas.

Because I was really busy with work and home life, we communicated via text or audio snippets. I "graduated" to telehealth appointments pre-pandemic before telehealth was widely accepted. Over time we moved off the platform and began to meet in person. Even though I could have been matched with anyone in the nation, I happened to be matched with someone who lived in Chicago and our daughters went to the same elementary school—a happy coincidence.

She is still my therapist years later and has seen me through some of my darkest times. She has helped me reframe my experiences and work through the untrue thoughts and negative self-talk in my head, provided tips to lessen my anxiety, and really just been in my corner and provide an objective (professional) perspective to help me in life. Therapists are lifesavers for people who suffer from ongoing anxiety, depression, or PTSD.

She believes everyone needs therapy, including children, especially now with the collective trauma we've experienced with the pandemic and current societal environment. She explained people usually come to therapy because of one problem, and that one thing reflects their inability to cope with other issues in life.

As you move through the stages of therapy, the goal is to get to the maintenance phase. In this phase, you maintain the new status quo and remind yourself of how much progress you've made. But that doesn't mean you don't regress. That's common. While you still will get knocked down, you shouldn't get knocked out.

I am in the maintenance phase of my therapy. I'm tweaking the rules of my life and acquiring new skills to avoid a relapse. I'm always learning new things. I'm better equipped to anticipate the situations in which a relapse may occur and have my toolbox to cope at the ready. What I'm striving for is personally worthwhile and meaningful. I'm patient with myself and can more easily recognize that healing is a work in progress, that I can let go of what held me back, move forward with something new, and find joy in the journey.

When do you know you are finished with therapy? My therapist said, "Therapy is not meant to be a board game and get to the finish, and cash in and win. Parents don't set a child free when they turn eighteen." Maintenance looks different for each person. Some people need booster shots at life transitions like marriage, death, and birth. Ultimately, it's up to you when you are done.

FINDING SPIRITUAL ADVISORS

We all have a component to us that no one else can see but feel in our hearts or in the core of our being. It's our soul. Whether you believe in a religion or no religion, we are all spiritual beings, and we can enrich our souls (and deplete our souls) with our bodies and minds. They are all connected.

God is important in my life. I am a Christian. and I rely on God for strength and to help me in life. So I went to a local church and sought out the counsel of a wise woman who I had talked to previously. Becky, a wise grandmother, mother, and community counselor, was a pillar of strength and support who listened to me and helped me wrestle with the difficult questions I was struggling with at the time.

We decided to read a book together, *When People Are Big and God Is Small* by Edward T. Welch, and covered a chapter or two each week. The process of reading the book and talking to her about it was very healing, as I sorted out my people-pleasing ways and how they were detrimental to my well-being. It also brought me to the conclusion that the goal of life is to serve others, as God served us—to be like his image and not Lone Rangers.

Yoga was the other spiritual component, but I would also say it had a lot to do with my body and mind too. It helped immensely. When I practice yoga, all parts of me, body, mind, and spirit, are truly in sync. Study after study has shown the benefits of yoga and how it can help reduce anxiety and depression. For me, it is now part of my daily ritual. Whether it's ten minutes or sixty, I make it a priority to fit yoga into my day to get my body, mind, and spirit into sync. This is also called embodiment. It helps me be present, focused, and less anxious. It moves my emotions through my body as I practice, sometimes shedding tears, or relieving pain where I didn't know I had any.

My way to yoga is through YouTube and my local yoga studio, especially the program I did with Kelli, my "come-as-you-are" and "just notice" teacher. Through YouTube, I subscribe to a free channel led by Adriene Mishler. She invites her audience to "Find What Feels Good," and to "breathe love in, breathe love out." She started posting yoga videos under the name

"Yoga with Adriene" in 2012 and has since seen her subscriber base explode to more than ten million, including me.

In an article titled "The Reigning Queen of Pandemic Yoga," she explained to the *New York Times*, "We're creating a space where it's not just safe but encouraging people to commit to the practice of self-discovery, versus just doing something that's good for you because you're *told* it's good for you."

Mishler sees her practice as a welcoming, loving alternative to traditional Western-style yoga where you have to sweat and burn hundreds of calories to feel like you've done a "real" workout that's good for you.

Doing a daily practice with Mishler helped me get stronger, mentally, and physically, through the pandemic, through my valley, and beyond. Yoga is helping millions of others too, like fitness guru Denise Austin.

As someone who has tried every workout under the sun in her decades-long career in fitness, Austin decided to take up yoga later in life. She told *Prevention* magazine in an article about exercise tips for mood swings, "I felt more anxious during my menopausal years, so I did more yoga and it helped me. Yoga is a great way to ease your nervous system and relieve lower back pain and neck tension."

The fitness instructor added that for women who are not super active, yoga is a great way to begin exercise because it's low impact. "You can also practice yoga outside, in a studio, or at home with online classes, so it can be pretty flexible with your schedule," she said.

But the soul can be fed in so many ways. I talk about that more in the next chapter.

FINDING OTHER EXPERTS AND ADVISORS

Another key element of your team is people who are experts in their field and who make you look, feel, and be your best. This could be someone who helps you eat better, exercise, or be your creative best. I'd also count people like your personal trainer, or people who help you excel in areas of your life where you couldn't otherwise (e.g., financial advisor, work mentors, teachers).

I also count my hairdresser as part of my team. Enissa, of Enshe Style in Chicago, is a talented beautician who performs her art on my hair three or four times a year. The partial highlight coloring process takes about three hours with my haircut, and during this time we pontificate about the world and its problems. A former nurse and philosophical Bosnian war veteran who has had her share of curve balls in life, Enissa helps me look better on the outside and feel good about myself. She also listens to me and allows me to share my thoughts and feelings without judgment. It's a version of talk therapy in a different chair. Hairstylists are magicians and therapists. They make you feel good inside and out.

There's also Judith, a talented artist and my watercolor teacher, who invited me to put aside my "shoulds" and simply create. These are some of the other people on my team who gently guided me to be my best self, but also help center me and discover parts of myself I didn't know existed.

CREATE YOUR OWN TEAM

Having a team can help you get through hard times, especially when you don't know what to do, or the next step to take. When we face the unknown, people make it a little more bearable to move forward. I'm so thankful for mine.

"Rarely, if ever, are any of us healed in isolation," wrote the late Gloria Jean Watkins, better known by her pen name bell hooks, an American author, professor, feminist, and social activist who passed away in 2021. "Healing is an act of communion."

I know that now more than ever. People need people to survive and to thrive.

CHAPTER 8 QUESTIONS:

1. Do you have a team? Who are the members? Take some time to reflect on who your people are. Consider writing them a thank you let them know the important role they play in your life.

2. Who are the friends who have your back? Do you listen to the advice they give you?

3. How can you make new friends? Have you made a new friend recently? How did you connect? What do you do for fun with them?

4. Do you know what a life coach or executive coach is? Have you used one before? Why or why not?

5. Do you have a therapist? Would you consider seeing one? Why or why not?

6. Do you have any people you consider to be spiritual advisors in your life? Who are they? Is there room to explore or add any others? Why or why not?

7. Who can help you live a better, whole life—or work to your potential? Who do you need to add to your team?

CHAPTER 9

Listen to the Universe

"If you want to find the secrets of the universe, think in terms of energy, frequency, and vibrations."

— NIKOLA TESLA

Philosophers, poets, scientists—lovers, fighters—humans of every age and background have all pondered the vastness and wonders of the universe at some point in their lives. Where do we come from? How did we get here? Where are we going? What is my part in this big, crazy, unknown place?

The Bible says in Hebrews 11:3, "By faith, we understand that the universe was created by the word of God, so that what is seen was not made out of things that are visible."

How do we make sense out of things that are not visible, like spirituality and the universe?

When I ponder the secrets of the universe and how I might tap into its vastness and energy, I think about Nikola Tesla. An engineer, physicist, and rival of Thomas Edison, Tesla was known for his lifelong study and discoveries in the production, transmission, and application of electricity. He believed the secrets of the universe were hidden in energy, frequency, and vibrations.

Living things consist of energy—especially humans. Perhaps that is one of the many reasons we feel comfort around other living things, other humans—but also animals like dogs and cats and plants, trees, flowers, and other things in nature. We commune with the energy, and somehow that brings us peace and helps center us.

Tesla's philosophy helps explain that which cannot be explained. One PhD student in wireless communications and electrodynamics, Amartansh Dubey, said of Tesla's theory, "Our perception of reality and all our technologies are directly or indirectly related to waves and parameters like frequency and energy. We are interacting with the current objective reality around us by seeing and listening to it because our eyes and ears can convert electromagnetic (light) and mechanical (sound) waves into electric neural signals interpreted by our brain. In fact, our brain firing, or decoding, neurons is an example of electrical impulses/ waves. So our perception of reality is based on our ability to decode/encode information in the waves."

He said our reality, time, gravity, vision, hearing, feelings (inside our brain), everything is related to waves. Whether we want to unravel secrets of the subatomic world or image supermassive black holes, all we need is to understand the behavior of waves.

On a more practical level, I often think of emotions coming to me in waves, especially the harder ones, like grief, shame, anxiety, and depression. Sometimes I feel like I'm drowning in the wave especially if it is a tsunami. Eventually, the wave dissipates, and it's calm again. Like the ocean of life. Sometimes I feel I'm in rough, choppy waters, holding on to a buoy for survival. I know I just have to make it through the moment (or moments) to get through to the calmer waters. The promise of a calmer sea is what gets me through challenging times.

Another way to think of Tesla's quote is that all of the universe is made up of energy that vibrates at different frequencies. I believe some of us can feel this universal energy, or tune into it and listen to it, better than others. But we all have it. Anyone or anything that is alive has it.

Some believe positive thoughts or energy can influence outcomes in a positive way, whereas negative thoughts or energy can have the opposite effect. Research has found a strong link between positive thinking and better health outcomes in a series of conditions including heart disease, traumatic brain injuries, stroke, and brain tumors. According to the Mayo Clinic, research has also linked positive thinking to:

- Increased life span
- Lower rates of depression
- Lower levels of distress
- Greater resistance to the common cold
- Better psychological and physical well-being
- Better cardiovascular health and reduced risk of death from cardiovascular disease

- Better coping skills during hardships and times of stress

The reason why is a little more unclear. The fact remains, positivity can lead to better outcomes in health and life.

So how can you tap into this energy—this part of us, other living things, and the universe--that we cannot see? This is the spiritual part of us, the part that requires faith, meditation, and/or quiet reflection. We must quiet our monkey mind so that we can be open to the energy, the vibration, and the waves that surround us.

Some people see this as God or a universal life force. In the *Star Wars* movies, they call it "The Force."

I have felt it in different ways all of my life, whether it be different people coming into and out of my life at the exact right time or the coincidences you just can't explain. I've felt the power of prayer and felt comforted by God. I've felt loved ones who've passed on around me. Again, it's not something I can entirely explain—it's just something I feel. I know other people feel it too.

HOPE'S STORY, PART I

Hope is a forty-three-year-old, successful Northwestern University journalism grad who was born north of Chicago to Jamaican parents. She has experienced the depths of grief, but also the power of the universe. One particularly hard stop sign in her life she shared with me when I spoke with her in December 2021 was the premature birth and passing of her twins in 2012, Cole and Ava.

In the cold, dark, and gray days of a Chicago November, Hope was nearly six months pregnant when she went into unexplained premature labor, and nothing could be done to stop it—even though she lived across the street from a hospital.

I got to hold my son and watch him pass, and then deliver my daughter, and watch her pass. I didn't know how I was going to survive. Every fiber of my body wanted to be with my children. I still don't know how I got through it. It was a void. I just put one step in front of the next. I would manage to get through the day and go to bed. My hormones were fluctuating wildly. My milk came in with no babies to feed. It was complete hell for me and the darkest time of my life.

When she left the hospital with empty arms, she said she felt completely alone. Even though her mom and sister were supportive and had also experienced premature birth, her husband soon returned to work, and she felt lost. She took several weeks off and started to attend weekly grief therapy. But the one thing that helped her heal was the opportunity to help others in her same situation.

I knew about March of Dimes' work to prevent premature birth after my nephew was born at twenty-six weeks. Instead of people sending me flowers, I ended up channeling my grief through having people make donations in memory of my twins. Every time someone made a donation, I'd get a card in the mail, acknowledging the contribution in their names. It felt good to see their names. It really kept me going.

I would think, Maybe this one will be the one dona-
tion that will help fund the research so that no mom
has to go through this again. It will be the one that
unlocks the mystery of premature birth. It will save
another mom from going through the grief I went
through. It really provided meaning to my tragedy.

She felt the power of the positive thoughts and energy others sent her way. "I was surprised how many people contributed," she said, recounting the gifts of coworkers, counterparts at the World Health Organization and the CDC, people who she connected with through her work and community. "I thought, 'Maybe this isn't just something horrible that happened to me. Maybe it will lead to something better.' It made me a beacon for other moms. So many baby loss moms have reached out and thanked me for being open. They've experienced similar things: stillbirth, late-term miscarriage, a genetic issue. All these moms were coming forward," she said. She found herself part of the baby loss mom community.

She looks at the people and opportunities that have come into her life, and she doesn't think they are coincidences.

Hope believes the universe brought her together with other baby loss moms to help her find meaning in her loss and help her move through life with support. She met a woman who suffered the passing of a baby girl due to preeclampsia, two months before Hope's twins were born. They couldn't save her and the baby, so they saved her. A few months later, the two women ran into each other at a local restaurant. By then Hope had her first rainbow baby in a baby carrier on her chest. Her friend opened her coat to reveal she too was having a rainbow baby and was pregnant with a girl.

They now have beautiful, healthy daughters three months apart. "We belong to a group that no one wants to be a part of but are able to support each other. I think it's fate. I feel like the universe puts people in your path for a reason. You can't explain it. We knew of each other, but never connected until our losses," she said.

Now, the family lives down the street from her and the girls play with each other.

She said she and her friend don't hide their shared loss from their rainbow babies. "We're very open with them. They are part of our family. My twins would be nine years old now—two years older than my daughter, who is two years older than my son. It has purpose and meaning. It wasn't just a tragedy that happened to take my life apart; it pulled me toward my purpose. Every time I share it, I have the chance to help other moms."

How did she find the strength to share her story? "I was bolstered once I started giving it purpose. When I started getting those cards and assigning meaning to something tragic," she said. But first, she had to let herself feel the grief. But she became more resilient by finding meaning in the loss by helping others. Then it snowballed.

"You're able to help yourself little by little. Then as you see that what you're doing is helping other people and changing other people's lives and you become a light to others. You know, that helps you keep going," she said.

DEFINING SPIRITUALITY

Hope grew up in the Episcopal church, went every Sunday, and had a big church family, largely an extended Caribbean family. As she's grown older, she said her spirituality has changed. She has leaned more into her own spirituality and believes in a higher power—whether it be the universe or God, she said it's the same to her. "It's the way of things. I've started to reconnect with my ancestors, the people who came before and surrounded me. I'm the first person in my family born in this country. I always feel like my grandfather was with me. I feel his presence, even though he died before I was born."

Although her twins and grandfather are no longer here, she said, "They are real people and real souls. They are with me. I feel my children are with me. If you let your guard down, you can feel them and know they are there. Loved ones surround you. That can be your inner voice."

Hope also has a strong interest in genealogy and has been able to learn more about her diverse heritage. Through her research, she's gotten to know her ancestors by seeing their pictures, names, and where they lived. She believes that when you can piece your story together you can start to see how your ancestors are part of your journey and that they want to see you win. "Being a woman of color, I know I come from both those who enslaved others and those who were enslaved—it's complicated. I found out my mom's grandma was Jewish. You see yourself as not just as you, but as part of a larger story, and that's fascinating."

Learning more about her background gives her purpose and comfort, and knowing their trials and tribulations gives her the foundation and strength to process and move through the inevitably uncomfortable parts of life. It roots her in the storms of life.

SIT WITH DISCOMFORT

"I'm not a particularly religious person," said Molly. "But I've always turned to concepts of Buddhism to get through hard times. I've learned to just sit with the discomfort, learn from it, and get through it. I'm understanding that discomfort is a part of life."

Of leaving her high-powered PR job at Microsoft to hang out in the unknown and find what's next, she said, "This is where I need to be. I need to be calm and listen to the universe. I find that's when things really fall in your lap. There's been a couple of things that have actually happened. This was from just being quiet and just waiting without asking the universe to give me signs. I didn't go in seeking things out and forcing things to happen, which I feel like can be a recipe for disaster, especially in times like these."

Not having control can feel really uncomfortable. We are taught to push through uncomfortable things to get to a better circumstance instead of listening to our bodies and sitting with the discomfort, then working to bring ourselves back to center.

Molly said, "It's like my swim coach in high school. Like, you know what, you have the flu, but that's your body. If you listen to your mind and tell yourself, you can swim through it. That's such an unhealthy mindset. But it's really how we're conditioned to push through it, to control your destiny, only you're in charge, which, frankly, you're still in charge of your destiny. You're just not forcing it. It's a very Western way of thinking to push through and ignore your body."

"Some of the Western stuff is okay," she said, "but maybe let it happen instead of working so hard to make it happen."

But in order to get back to center and release our anxiety and sense of control, we really need to let it go. We need to learn to live Elsa's anthem in the animated Disney blockbuster *Frozen*—to let it go. Or as many Christians say, "Let go and let God." In either case...the main lesson is to let it go. Trust the universe. Trust God. Trust your true self.

MY STORY, YOUR STORY

How has the universe played a role in my life? I've seen messages and signs multiple times. Some are more apparent than others. I find it's hard for the universe to get my attention because I'm so stubborn and want to control things and so some intense things happen to stop me in my tracks.

The universe stopped my crazy path to self-destruction with a freak January blizzard. The universe stopped my path to self-destruction and tight hold on security and my ego by helping me leave a toxic workplace, a few times over. With each stop sign the universe, or God, throws in my path, new opportunities arise. From a broken vessel, new and beautiful things can be made.

I feel like God spoke to me, in an audible alto in my head, once. It was when I lost my firstborn, Faith Lily. I distinctly remember driving on Lake Shore Drive. It was cold and dark. I sat in the passenger seat of our Nissan, with my husband steering the black sedan toward the hospital. I was so distraught. I heard a commanding, otherworldly voice in my head. It spoke clearly, purposefully. One simple sentence. A promise. "There will be others," it told me, a first-time mom whose heart was breaking. There were. The voice spoke the truth.

As I've been writing this book, I've been presenting myself in different ways to my family, friends, and colleagues—putting some positive vibes out into the universe, if you will. I've found that with more positivity more frequently, the energy vibrating back has been positive. It's a little physics—every action has an equal and opposite reaction. You put out good energy, you get good energy back. Put out negative energy, negative energy returns. Karma.

When it comes to spirituality, be intentional about your energy. Be intentionally aware. Intentionally direct and give positive energy. Intentionally receive positive energy and reject negative energy. Intentionally just be.

How?

You can do this through physical movement, like running or hiking; through creative expression, like art or music;

through service, like volunteering or donating; through hobbies like gardening, photography, or birdwatching.

During my recovery, I took a virtual watercolor painting class through my local botanic garden. I went on a weekend trip to Florida by myself where I went to the beach, painted, and biked the Pinellas Trail. I went hiking with my best friends in Colorado. I continued to volunteer as a leader for my Girl Scout troop. I helped our local ballet studio navigate the unknowns of COVID-19 to remain open. I spent time with my kids, going for coffee or on walks. I went on dinner dates with my husband.

Work on positive self-talk. Surround yourself with positive people. Reframe negative situations. Laugh more.

Do something to be quiet. Meditate. Pray. Go be in nature. Go to church or another place of worship.

Meditation doesn't have to be hard or take a lot of time. It can be as simple as closing your eyes, no matter where you are, and taking a few deep breaths.

It can be uncomfortable. But sit with your discomfort, whether it's five minutes, five hours, or five days.

Take the time to invest in listening to the universe. You won't regret it.

CHAPTER 9 QUESTIONS:

1. What do you think Tesla's quote means?

2. What does spirituality mean to you?

3. How do you tap into the energy of God or the universe? When does God/it speak to you?

4. What do you do to be quiet, reflect, be in the moment?

5. Has anything happened to you that you haven't been able to explain?

CHAPTER 10

Let Go and Make Space

———

"With life as short as a half taken breath, don't plant anything but love."

— RUMI

Breathing is the foundation of life.

Breathing in is spontaneous.

Breathing out is spontaneous.

We breathe, in and out, rhythmically like the waves in the ocean, coming and going.

Air suddenly arrives and then simply departs. According to Johns Hopkins Medicine, the average adult breathes twelve to sixteen times each minute.

We can try and hold our breath and control it, but eventually it falls back into the same pattern all humans and living beings share.

Breath is something we ultimately can't control. It just *is*.

Concentrating on it can make us more aware, more present.

Breath replicates the cycle of life and new beginnings—taking in and letting go and making space for fresh air and energy to renew us.

Throughout life, we can get stuck, in jobs, relationships, clutter, bad habits—dark places. It can feel stifling. Overwhelming. Hopeless. Like we can't breathe, and we don't even know how to take the first step to get unstuck. But I go back to the breath. Focus on breathing, in and out. The promise of life, and a new beginning, over and over.

The first step is letting go and making space for a new beginning.

So how did I do that? How do you do that?

My anchor is my breath, my breath is my anchor.

LET GO OF THE "SHOULD"
We are not our "shoulds."

I should lose twenty pounds.

I should work out more.

I should be a better parent or friend.

I should spend more time with my family.

I should be in a better relationship.

I should be making more money.

I should live in a nicer house. Drive a nicer car.

What if the only "should" we "should" be is to be centered? To be our authentic self? To love ourselves and love one another. And when we mess up, to forgive? Wouldn't the rest of the "shoulds" not matter? It would be okay to be perfectly imperfect, to try to be the best we can be, and forgive ourselves when we feel less than, and then try again the next day.

But how do we get to this point where we can live centered, present and just be enough as we are? It's a continual process of letting go and making space for the things that bring us closer to who we really are and get us closer to our highest purpose or sense of self. Not the place where we live in "should" and "less than."

I feel like the "should" is especially hard in a capitalistic, social media-driven American society where success is often measured by your accomplishments, be it your grades, your awards, your career, your looks, your income, or things you own. Or where you vacation, your kids, their accomplishments. Not as much recognition is given to those who take the path less traveled—the kind, the humble, the tenderhearted, the not-so-showy—those who just are, without caring about accolades and praise from others.

THE PRICE OF "SHOULD"

Look at how we treat our caretakers of society: our healthcare workers, our teachers, our parents. Many of these people are women. We've given up so much of ourselves to achieve what we think we "should" be doing to please others. We've said no to ourselves so many times at the expense of our soul. Women do it so much—in our twenties, in our thirties, in our forties—year after year until your body rebels finally, and says, "Hey, when are you gonna listen to me? You can't do this anymore!"

In January 2021 my body finally had enough and said, "I've listened to you for so long. You've pushed me to the side over and over again. You didn't go to the bathroom so you could write 'just one more email' too many times. You stayed up until 2 or 3 a.m. to work one too many times. You've said yes one too many times. I am done. I am done. I am done. You're asking me to put this other thing that just happened to you off to the side? No. You need to deal with this, friend. Listen to me."

My body took me by my brain and shook it—hard. "You listen, missy. Yeah, we're done with it. This is the path to nowhere."

It was the total toddler hissy fit you cannot ignore no matter how hard you try. It's the annoying whining you cannot tune out.

So why do we do it? Why do we ignore our bodies? Maybe it's because we don't want to deal with what it might be saying to us. Or it's because we think it's what we should do. It's the American way. If you work hard, you play hard.

You do all the things that you're supposed to do, all the way through. I always got good grades because I got rewarded. Then I went to a good college, and then I got a good job. I was successful, at least by society's standards, and I liked it. But I did it at the expense of everything else—my mental health, my relationships.

It was a workaholic thing. You know, work hard, play hard. Work took priority over everything. It was something I could control, was good at, and was rewarded for. I couldn't help myself. Then I looked at other people. Maybe some of my friends were able to cut themselves off and say, "That's enough. I'm gonna go and rest." I looked at them as weak or not as tough as me. Maybe they had it right all along.

So to get through to a more authentic me, I needed to let go of my workaholic ways and my desire for security and just be. I needed to chill out and focus on the most important things and the rest will come. I needed to listen to my authentic self, listen to my tribe, and listen to the universe. Listen to God. I just needed to trust and let go of my fears and the feelings of "I am less than or imperfect if I rest." I am enough.

What do you need to let go of to move toward your authentic self? What stands in your way? What is blocking your energy?

Your body will tell you when it's time to stop and let go. Or a life circumstance will. Melissa said when it happens, "Lean into the full stop. Don't just see a stop sign and roll through it. Really stop. Sleep a lot. Get healthy. Get calm. Try not to be triggered. I needed to not be triggered. It's a very triggering world right now."

PURSUE PEACE: HOPE'S STORY, PART II

Hope moved away from the things that weren't working in her life and intentionally moved toward peace. That meant letting go of her marriage and forging a new path with her young children. It was extremely painful and courageous to take these steps, but it left space for new things to happen and moved her toward her true self and less pain and suffering.

"In 2019, it was a tumultuous time in my home life. As soon as I let go of what was emotionally holding me down, all these opportunities started flooding in. In February 2019, right after I got separated, I wrote an article on my twins for *InStyle* and did an *NPR* interview about the healthcare disparity of women of color experiencing premature birth and post-birth hemorrhage," she explained.

Her twins' birth story captured the attention of an Illinois legislator, who asked Hope to testify about her experience in front of a committee. "I had to repeatedly ask for a blood transfusion in the hospital, even though their own system had flagged my hemoglobin levels as critical. My mom was with me—she worked in the ER for forty years and that day she advocated for me to get a transfusion. But they wouldn't listen to us. The healthcare committee reviewed a bill to establish a mechanism to help prevent postpartum hemorrhage."

She spoke of two other high-profile women who are black who also had difficult birth stories—Beyoncé and Serena Williams—and said they're good examples of the healthcare disparity facing moms of color. In fact, according to the CDC, Black women are three times more likely to die from a pregnancy-related cause than White women. She hopes that raising awareness will help to change that.

"Two people on the committee cried," she remembered about that day in Springfield, where her mom stood by her side again. The committee passed the bill. She told herself afterward, "That happened to you because you have the ability to turn it into positive change." And she's proud of that.

Through the loss of her twins and the breakup of her marriage, Hope continued to pursue peace. She tries to create an oasis in every part of her life. In her new home, she said, "I made it a peaceful space, and while spending so much time at home during the pandemic, it has given me so much clarity. It's absolutely where I'm supposed to be."

And the house she lives in now?

When I went to see the house, I recognized the faces in a picture frame as retirees who knew my dad. I feel like this was supposed to be my house. I've renovated it in colors that are inviting and warm. I've become intentional about who I let in my space and how I talk about the space to my kids. My kids and I do centering exercises. We breathe and do meditation. We set daily intentions. It's a practice. I'm very intentional with parenting and creating a peaceful space.

She further explained, "It's not in my temperament to have strife. During the more tumultuous times, I wanted to prioritize peace more. The strife was impacting my health. I was having panic attacks. My blood pressure was sky high."

She knew she wanted something different. It started as a thought—then it became an intention.

The concept of creating a peaceful space throughout her life became her guiding star. Now, if something doesn't bring her peace, then she doesn't prioritize it. "Peace is my barometer." She shared a story of how she bought a pretty Christmas tree with glitter for $30 online, shaking her head side to side. "There was glitter everywhere. It wouldn't stand up straight. It was making me crazy and filled me with anxiety. It wasn't worth it." Since it didn't bring her peace, she threw it away and got a real tree. "Such a simple solution, done with intention."

She released what wasn't working to welcome in something new.

As difficult as getting a divorce was, she was able to move on, which allowed her to make space for love again. "My partner now—he is smart, emotionally intelligent, and he provides emotional support. He cheers for me and pushes for me in a way I didn't have before. He supports and encourages me. He opens my eyes to things I'm blind to about myself. It's nice to have someone like that in your corner."

Her new partner, a friend from college who played on her university football team, is a French-speaking Canadian. He was based in China for his job as an educational consultant. They had been friends on Facebook for many years but reconnected in a casual conversation after her separation. A phone call led to a weekend meetup when he came to the Chicago area, which eventually blossomed into a long-distance romance. With the geographic difference, it wasn't a relationship she was seeking, or even a possibility in her mind.

To think someone who lives in Shanghai would arrange their schedule to repeatedly come to see me seven thousand miles away is not in the realm of possibility for me. It's refreshing to be with someone who means and does what they say. There's no scenario where this makes sense, but it's happening. Since we reconnected, he's transitioned into a job in the US. It somehow just all makes sense. I have a minor in French from Northwestern and he's fluent in French. He has Caribbean parents like me. He cooks Caribbean food that we both love. We both love international travel and have similar tastes in music. There is a shared cultural currency. He was a sociology major, I minored in anthropology—we look at things similarly."

Shaking her head framed by her tight, blonde, crew-cut curls, she said, "I didn't expect this—I wasn't looking for this relationship, but I really embrace it. It doesn't have to seem plausible to become real."

Ahh, the universe. Lovely things happen when we go with the flow.

FORCE VS. FLOW

Breathing, in order to work smoothly, should not be forced. It can be painful, and even deadly if it is forced. It works best when it flows.

It's like life. If you are pushing hard for things to happen, especially if it is from a place of "should" or a place of lacking, it will never be enough.

My wise, gorgeous inside-and-out friend Matty May, fifty, a vice president of sales for Paramount and life coach, said, "If you get in the flow, you're coming from a place of abundance. Then you are not fighting for what is missing, rather you are powered forward with all you do have."

People who operate from a place of abundance can rest and pause because they know they can keep going and aren't afraid of losing anything—they can face their fears.

Like US gymnast Simone Biles. She didn't force herself to compete in the 2021 Tokyo Olympics, even though she was favored to win multiple medals and break records. When she took a break from the competition to take care of her mental health, she said, "No, this is enough." She knew she needed a break and needed to take care of herself. Then she came back when she was ready and was still able to perform for herself—and no one else. She didn't feel like she had to force herself into getting a gold medal.

Part of America was rooting for her. But another part shouted, "What a quitter!" I was rooting for her. She moved from a place of flow.

Part of the reason I had my breakdown is my identity was so wrapped in what I did for a living. It was my safe space— where I could excel and be recognized and rewarded for my efforts. So when that was called into question a few times in my career, it was followed by a breakdown. I wasn't resilient enough to separate myself from my work—and I wasn't able to center myself and regain balance in chaos in other ways. I've always reset myself through my work, not through looking at who I was at my core—forgiving myself, moving on, and resetting it. It was all or nothing. Success or failure. Nothing in between.

To have a mindset where I'm open to starting over and being vulnerable is a gift. I don't have to keep the baggage of my career failures (or any failure, for that matter). My career is not linear, and it doesn't define me. So I don't need to have a massive breakdown if I stop on that path—it shouldn't be a big deal. I was angry at myself for allowing my breakdown to wipe me out so hard. A job shouldn't do that.

I was forcing my job because I thought that was who I should be, and it defined who I am. But my perfect day involves so many things outside of my job. Do I need to worry so much about paying the bills to get it all? Earning a living is important, but it doesn't have to be my everything.

LIVING IN THE MARGINS
Part of being compassionate to others involves being compassionate with yourself. Make space to give yourself something—energy, sleep, a walk—before you give to others. Put your oxygen mask on first before you put it on others. If you don't, you can eventually burn out.

But how do we do this? And find the time? How can we let go and make space in our lives, in big and small ways? Whether you need to leave something or someone or make more time for yourself, it all starts with a simple step or thought, with an intention.

Professors Peter M. Gollwitzer and Gabriele Oettingen of the Motivation Lab at New York University are experts on a self-regulatory strategy called "implementation intentions." Studies show people are more likely to do something when they specify how, when, and where they will do it—in other words, when they are intentional.

One of the first steps is to plan a space for them in your life: Altering your environment so your water bottle or glass has a place to sit. Somewhere to put your book, your journal, your running shoes…just like where you plan for your guest to sit when they visit. You're letting yourself know that something new is welcome; you are giving it a place and energy to exist.

When you live in the margins, you create space in your daily life to allow for yourself to just be and to welcome new energy into your life—to recharge yourself so you don't burn out, or to have the energy to try new things. This can look like not booking appointments or activities back-to-back and leaving a fifteen- to thirty-minute window in between. Or intentionally carve out a few minutes a day for "me" time.

Be intentional about including "margin" time in your day. Is it in the morning? At night? Before your morning coffee? At lunch? Whatever it is, set aside the time. In that time, do what you need to do to give yourself energy: Rest. Read. Journal. Breathe.

If you've ever tried to slip a playing card into a tightly packed box, you'll know how a change feels when it's being forced. If you've shuffled cards, you've seen space emerge when you allow them to bend and breathe. Then when you slip a card into the pack, it slides right in. Living in the margins allows you to rest, renew, and create time and space to breathe.

A FEW WORDS ABOUT REDEMPTION

Sometimes things happen in life where we don't show up as our best selves. We hurt others—whether intentionally or unintentionally—or they hurt us. Or sometimes we hurt ourselves with destructive behaviors and habits. How do we move on from this hurt? One word: forgiveness.

"The weak can never forgive. Forgiveness is the attribute of the strong," said Mahatma Gandhi in his book *All Men are Brothers: Autobiographical Reflections.*

Whether you need to forgive yourself or someone else or ask for forgiveness from someone or God, just do it. Forgiveness releases stuck destructive negative energy and can free you to move on and be renewed. It is so simple but so hard. Do it with intention and a pure heart and see what happens. It can be life changing.

In Christianity, we talk a lot about forgiveness. That's what it means to be "born again." We ask God to forgive us because his son Jesus died for our sins. It's a free gift to anyone who wants to accept it. If someone wrongs us, we are to turn the other cheek. We are to love our neighbor as ourselves. Buddha taught that learning to live a life that embraces forgiveness could be achieved through repeated meditation (Moffitt, 2022). Muslims believe that Allah is merciful and forgiving and that humans can and should forgive too (Gusau, 2021).

However you arrive at forgiveness, it is a spiritual practice, and a difficult one, as it often involves overcoming pride, hurt, anger, and resentment. But if you can embrace it, the path forward is so much more joyful and free. You have the freedom to live a perfectly imperfect life and move closer to your authentic self.

CHAPTER 10 QUESTIONS:

1. Where in your life are you stuck? What is causing you to be stuck?

2. How can you move through this obstacle? Who or what can help you?

3. What would your life look like if you let go and became unstuck?

4. Can you remember a time in your life when you were in the "flow"? When was it? How did you feel? How do you think your life would be different if you lived with more flow than force?

5. What does living in the margins mean to you? How can you incorporate this concept into your daily life?

6. What does forgiveness mean to you? Is there anyone you need to forgive? Or is there something you need to ask forgiveness for? How can you make amends?

PART FOUR

FIND JOY IN THE JOURNEY

CHAPTER 11

Embrace the New You

"Take the first step in faith. You don't have to see the whole staircase, just take the first step."

— MARTIN LUTHER KING, JR.

So, now what? The tools and resources I've outlined thus far helped me rebuild and establish a solid foundation. They've helped me continue on my journey a little more mindfully, a little lighter, with more intention and a little more resilience. I hope some of these tools and resources may do the same for you.

I've embraced a new me—a whole me—my authentic self in body, mind, and spirit. Maybe you have too. Or maybe you are doing it again, for the second time or the twenty-second time. The truth is, we remake ourselves many times in our lives. Sometimes we do it in big ways as we venture down new paths, sometimes in small ways. That's the gift of a journey, you can start over or go back to the beginning multiple times. Every day is a new day, a new beginning. I am more than my failures or shortcomings. You are too.

Melissa said about remaking herself over the past three decades, "In years when I was plugging along, I wanted to figure out how to create a life authentic to me and do something I really care about, so I took baby steps toward it. I tried many different degree programs: Social work. Psychology. Art therapy. Things would happen that would stop me. But I know my truth. I know I want to help people. And I will help people until I am eighty. So I am always looking for that."

What does embracing the new you look like?

For Hope, she learned to accept her intuition. She is learning to tap more into her inner voice through Reiki, which according to the Cleveland Clinic is "an energy healing technique that promotes relaxation, reduces stress and anxiety through gentle touch." It is used around the world to complement other forms of health treatment and comes from the Japanese words rei, meaning "universal," and ki, which refers to the vital life force energy that flows through all living things.

Her Reiki practitioner was very intuitive. Not only has this experience helped Hope understand and accept her own intuition, but it's also helped heal her. "After I've done Reiki, I feel lighter." Hope smiled. "I still talk to a therapist. That helps me. It helps me keep things in perspective. It helps you to have that have some checks and balances."

For Molly, she's learning to pay attention to her body more. "I've always listened to my mind and thought that pain was something to be pushed through. This is a metaphor for leaving the corporate world—my brain fog was a warning that something's wrong and I had to stop and slow down." Since she's left her job, she's working hard to tap into her inner curiosity and just notice how she is feeling. Focusing on the farm has helped clear her mind, as has keeping active with yoga, running, and Pilates.

Like Molly, I felt burnout at work. My other life responsibilities and the circumstances of the pandemic, and my lack of good coping skills to deal with it all sent me into a depression, and then over the edge. We both experienced a Great Awakening from the pandemic and then took part in the Great Resignation.

Like Molly, I realized I needed a time-out from my career to reassess. I needed to stop, figure out who I truly was, and rebuild so I could come back stronger and more resilient—so I could do hard things without falling apart. I needed space and time to explore and get reacquainted with my true self, and then utilize her to give back and serve others and take care of myself and my family.

Molly said a combination of things prompted her to reassess her life. "When everything in your life changes and the world around you is seemingly falling apart at the seams, there are moments when you just stop and think about what fundamentally matters and what you love and care about. As we rebuild our lives exiting the pandemic, what do we want that life to look like? I simply didn't want to be chained to a computer screen or Teams calls for twelve hours a day on the other side of it all."

During 2020, the only constant in my life was working. I couldn't see friends or family or do most of the things I normally do so there was a hyper-focus on two things: work as well as adapting and finding new pandemic-friendly hobbies and ways to stay connected. Through this, my love of being outdoors—running, hiking, backpacking, and taking care of my animals—went through the roof. I was at peace doing these things. I started noticing the contrast of how unhappy and anxious I was being tied to a computer screen. I was so curious about the outside world around me but had no curiosity left for the work of my job. I knew deep down things had to change somehow, but it took me over a year to actually do anything about it.

Molly noticed a lot of signs that she was suffering from burnout. "Foremost, I was frustrated and irritable for a good portion of the workweek. I had trouble concentrating. I was in a fog all the time at work. Tasks became tedious and pumping myself up to do pretty much any project was nearly impossible. I would count the minutes until meetings were over."

The former corporate cube-dweller is now a fledgling farmer. "I always joked during my time in corporate work that 'I'd rather be a farmer.' It was actually the headline of all my social media profiles for years."

While it may have been a joke at the time, she is now manifesting what she had in her profile. She's a year out of corporate work and still doesn't know if it'll be a full-time job or a hobby. Either way, she now has thirty-seven chickens, all new coops, two guard dogs who are big fluffy teddy bears, and several goats.

EMBRACE WHAT MAKES YOU HUMAN

Embracing the new me meant tapping into my creativity more. One of the things I learned along my journey is to recall what gives me joy—either now, or especially as a child. So I revisit those activities to live a life with meaning.

For me, that means doing more things where I can create. I am a creator.

I really enjoy painting, whether it be a Sip and Paint night out with my friends or leading my Girl Scout troop in a painting badge. There is something about a blank canvas and filling it with color and life that brings me joy. The same with writing. I love to fill words on a blank page or screen and tell stories or write poems, as I did when I was a schoolgirl.

I also like to take photos. I take hundreds, if not thousands, of photos every year—of my family, friends, trips, the beautiful and the mundane of everyday life. It's my way of documenting the moments of my time on earth and saving them to remember the sweetness and the sadness. It could be part of the journalist in me and my love of the visual arts. At the end of each year I make a calendar for my mom, my stepmom, and my mother-in-law. It brings me a lot of joy to remember and reflect on the past year, and then be hopeful for the new one ahead. They love the gift too. It's a win-win.

One of the subjects I most like to photograph, besides my children, is nature, especially flowers and trees. I'm drawn to their energy and beauty. That's probably why I also like to garden. I'm an amateur gardener, but every year (for the past twenty-plus years) I've created window boxes and container gardens. I love seeing the flowers and plants grow and change throughout the season. I love planting a seed and watching it go through the life cycle of living, bearing fruit or flowers, and then passing on—sometimes forever, sometimes until the next season. I love watching how trees or perennials grow from season to season. It gives me life to watch the circle of life and beauty of a garden.

We are more than what we do for a living, or for the people we care for in our lives. When I tap into my creative self, I feel the essence of what being human is. I am uniquely me.

It's unfortunate that arts in school are viewed in many circles as "extras." They should be seen as "essentials." They are essential to us being human and help us live life, no matter what comes our way. It helps us be resilient and work out things that cannot be explained when words are not enough. The arts live within each of us, whether it be music, visual arts, industrial arts, drama, dance, or something else. It's what makes us feel alive—and everyone should be given a chance to identify and develop their creativity and humanness. Mankind would be better for it. Maybe we'd have better mental health, and not be so reliant on antidepressants.

What part of the arts or being outdoors makes you feel alive? Brings you joy?

EMBRACE SACRED SPACES

As you embrace the new you, create or identify sacred places for yourself—a place to go that brings you joy. Maybe it's a comfy chair in your home. A special spot in your yard, or at a park. Or, like , your entire house. You probably have more than one.

I have several sacred places. I love to be by the water—any lake, river, stream, or ocean. Sometimes, even a swimming pool or bathtub will do. Specific places with water I love are Lake Michigan from downtown Chicago, the Gulf of Mexico from Clearwater Beach or Caladesi Island, and the cliffs in Cornwall, England, overlooking the Atlantic Ocean.

I'm a huge baseball fan. I love being next to a ball field and watching games. Whether it is watching my son or daughter playing softball or going to Wrigley Field, the cathedral of baseball, I am happy. I also enjoy watching my youngest daughter dart up and down the field playing soccer.

Gardens are sacred places for me. My favorite and most healing place is the Chicago Botanic Garden. I am at peace walking through a familiar place and experiencing the changing seasons, from the barren trees and snow-white landscapes of winter to the fresh green and pastels of renewed life in spring to the vibrant colors of summer to the crimson and orange of fall. It rejuvenates my soul.

Like many of my best friends, going on hikes in nature brings me strength and renewal. Whether it is a Midwestern hardwood forest in the dead of winter, golden aspens in Colorado in the fall, or pine forests with mountain views in the summer, trees are the army that guard my soul. They are upright soldiers that give me breath, literally and figuratively.

Listening to live music also brings me joy and peace. It can be my daughter performing on her clarinet with her high school marching band or playing the keyboard in her rock band, my other daughter playing her ukulele or guitar, or going to see my favorite musician or group live at a local venue like the Vic, the United Center, or Soldier Field. I especially love when it's a smaller venue and you can feel the beat of the music in your whole being. On another level, I love hearing singing bowls or chimes during a meditative yoga practice. The frequency resonates with my mind, body, and spirit.

These are just some of the places that bring me energy and renewal and allow me to feel centered, present, and alive—to just be. Where are your places?

EMBRACE HAPPY REMINDERS

When life gives you lemons, make lemonade. Life can be hard. But we can actively make a choice, every day, to find beauty no matter how dark things may seem.

As you embrace the new you, you will falter. But the new you will get back up and aim to realign yourself toward center, or your North Star. It can even be a small something that brings you back. Maybe it's a little memento, a gift from a loved one, a photo, that reminds you of your best you, love, or beauty.

I wear a ring on my finger to remember my lost child, Faith Lily, every day, and my wedding ring, to remind me of my love for my husband. I have small items in my home that remind me of my grandparents who have passed. I have a few paintings that either bring a smile to my face or my heart every time I look at them. I have an Airedale dog that has unconditional love for me and brings me joy. I look at my favorite Bible verses to remember I'm not alone.

One of my favorite verses that has sustained me is, "God is our refuge and strength, an ever-present help in trouble. Therefore we will not fear, though the earth give way and the mountains fall in the heart of the sea, though its waters roar and foam and the mountains quake with their surging," Psalms 46: 1-3, NIV.

EMBRACE GRATITUDE

As someone who suffers from anxiety, I consistently see, read, hear, etc. that practicing gratitude will help me. Every motivational speaker, psychologist, psychiatrist, or guru suggests it. So it must be true, right? Just do it!

What are you grateful for? I'm grateful for the roof over my head. I'm grateful for my family, my city, my nation, my world, no matter how broken or infuriating they can be.

Practicing gratitude helps me reframe my life and environment, remain centered, and find joy in the journey.

The poet Maya Angelou said she was grateful at every age. She practiced gratitude each morning, telling God: "Thank you for this day. Thank you for the light coming through the window. Thank you. Thank you that I'm breathing. Thank you. Thank you for everything. Thank you for the phone call that told me that I have the job. Thank you even for the phone call that told me I'm not wanted anymore. Thank you because I know you have something better for me lined up."

For someone who experiences anxiety, it's not easily "cured" with gratitude. Being grateful seems like a platitude sometimes. I'd say it's okay to not be okay. We need to sit with our discomfort. The best thing anyone can do for us in some instances is to sit with us, listen, and not try to solve anything. Just be. The way I feel cared for is if someone just listens.

Author of *Hold On, But Don't Hold Still: Hope and Humor from My Seriously Flawed Life,* Kristina Kuzmic shared this sentiment on Instagram: "So often I've heard people react to someone who is struggling with some version of 'What do you have to be anxious (or depressed) about? You have a great life! Just write down everything you're grateful for and think about that." Often those well-intentioned comments just add to the "what is wrong with me?' feelings, which are the last thing anyone who is struggling needs.

Yes, it's a wonderful, important, and even powerful practice to focus on all we're grateful for, but gratitude doesn't magically erase struggles. You can be incredibly grateful *and* anxious at the same time. You can be incredibly grateful *and* depressed at the same time.

Thankfully, I no longer wonder "what is wrong with me?" (I did, for years.) I no longer carry any guilt or shame for having struggles. Regardless of how some people try to portray their life, I am convinced every human being struggles with their mental health at some point, so why feel any embarrassment about it?

All that to say...in case you need to hear it today: give yourself room to feel what you feel, to feel a lot of different emotions, even the ones that may seem contradictory. There will always be someone who won't understand or empathize—that's not your problem, so put down that suitcase. If you're asking yourself "what is wrong with me?" the answer is: nothing. You are a feeling human in an overwhelming and complicated world. Find the tools, get the help, and learn what works best for you. I'm doing the same.

CHAPTER 11 QUESTIONS:

1. How are you embracing the new you? How do you reset yourself?

2. What part of the arts or being outdoors makes you feel alive? Brings you joy?

3. Where are your sacred spaces that give you energy and help you recharge?

4. What are items or people that bring a smile to your face?

5. What are you grateful for? How do you practice gratitude?

6. Where do you go when you want to process discomfort?

CHAPTER 12

The Journey

"Travel isn't always pretty. It isn't always comfortable. Some-times it hurts, it even breaks your heart. But that's okay. The journey changes you; it should change you. It leaves marks on your memory, on your consciousness, on your heart, and on your body. You take something with you. Hopefully, you leave something good behind."

— ANTHONY BOURDAIN

When you put together all of the previous chapters, you get a roadmap for my journey. My journey from breakdown to standing back up. If you hit a stop sign as I did, you need to get back up and rise again. Continue on the journey. It's not easy. But the world needs you, your story, and your light. Really. Every one of us is loved, and valuable. You are worthy. If you don't feel like you are that to anyone else, you are to God or the universe. You matter—no matter what.

When you hit a stop sign, take time to look and listen. Look inward—what is your body and mind telling you? Look outward—who can help you through your particular circumstance? Look upward—find a power greater than yourself to continue on your journey. Listen to your body, listen to the helpers you've identified, listen to a higher power. Identify people, places, and things that help center you and bring you joy and make time for yourself to live in the margins. Strive to be imperfectly perfect and let go of the "should." Embrace the new you and keep walking on the path of authenticity the best you can.

This book isn't about providing all of the answers. It's an outline of what helped me. To help you get started. You fill in the rest. These are tools to take with you on the roads you travel as you live your life—things to take with you to keep you on the road—or on top of the water, riding the waves, instead of crashing or drowning when the stop sign comes.

It's difficult to follow the road and walk on the journey. That's why we need help or tools—and ultimately, we need each other. *We cannot do it alone.* We are not designed that way.

While I was writing this book, my journey to recovery, better mental health, a better me...I came across other stop signs—crash and burn moments, or times I felt like I was drowning. So I activated my team and used the map I've outlined in this book to guide me along the path. That's the thing with people who struggle with mental health—we just seem to have more high highs and low lows, either in our head or in reality. I've felt like an imposter writing this at times, like, "Who am I to be writing a book on this topic?" or "Why do I want to put all this personal stuff about my life out there?"

In finishing this book, I came across a story about a pop star from the '90s, Darren Hayes. He has an incredible story of overcoming depression, suicidal ideation, and abuse and embracing his authentic self. He shares it so bravely, saying, "By speaking about what most embarrasses us, it's my hope that bringing light to sadness drives away the darkness." I feel the same way. I know everyone doesn't, though, and my wish for you is that you find the courage to share your truth.

I am in a different place than I was in January 2021. I've changed. I had gone to the depths and came out the other side. I know how to center myself—be resilient, feel emotions, my energy in motion. I can ride the waves of life. I know it's only temporary. I can look inward and take walks in nature, breathe, write in my journal. I can connect with others. I can look into the great beyond for answers. I lean on my people and on God, my refuge and strength. I practice yoga to feel embodied. I feel like I have more tools to observe the voice in my head more objectively, without judgment, and just be.

My job does not define who I am. It no longer determines my life—who I love and what I give to others in my day to day. I am more than that.

We can make mistakes and be sorry. I think there should be more room for forgiveness. It's a zero-tolerance world we are living in now, and I'm not sure that is right. Forgiveness is beautiful, necessary, and hard. Both for ourselves and others. I hope this book helps the readers do just that: forgive themselves and others on this journey, strive to live in the center, and serve and love others in order to make the world a better place. Amen.

Or as the Stoics would say: While you can't control what happens to you, you can control how you respond (Haden, 2022).

LAURA'S STORY

Laura Martinez, forty-six, is a mom of a tweenage daughter. A beautiful Latina and marathoner with a strong sense of self-worth, she's a former police officer who received a special commendation for saving a person who was jumping from a bridge to end their life. She's a current public teacher with a wicked sense of humor—a mama bear for her child, her cats, and her students. She recently lost her mother to kidney failure. She learned a lot from her mom and shared her words of wisdom about forgiveness with me when I interviewed her in June 2022.

> *My mom used to tell me, "Let bygones be bygones." She had so many examples to share, especially how she finally forgave her mother for leaving her father and three sisters for another love. Mom was the oldest and took on the role of caregiver to her dad who would suffer from epileptic seizures. She became a mom figure to her two younger sisters, making sure they ate, were clothed, and went to school. I would often wonder how she could forgive such a selfish act by someone who was supposed to be there to care for, protect and love her children. It did take many years for mom to have a relationship and work on forgiveness, but she did it.*

She continued,

Have you ever heard of the quote by Iman Ali, "For-giveness is the best revenge"? Well, that was me in a nutshell. I figured if someone wronged me then they needed punishment before I could ever even think of forgiving. I don't know why I became that person, but I felt I was someone who always had the best intentions and wouldn't hurt a soul. Why was I always the one who would end up upset, crying, and confused? Mom would give me that motherly advice, "Those friends weren't for you or that guy didn't know what he had." Yeah, those words that you don't want to hear when you are hurting.

It took me many years to fully understand all of the advice my mom gave me. As a teacher of preteens, I have taken on the role of their second mom. They confide in me with stories about their friends or their families. About their hardships, mistakes, times of anger, sadness, and all the unknown of their lives.

I share times when I too felt similar ways and give them advice on how to be grateful for what they have, to give themselves some space to fully understand the situation, and ways to forgive the ones who are upset-ting them. I tell them how their energy truly belongs to them and not to share their precious energy with anyone who does not deserve it. Sometimes they will then get angry with themselves, and I teach them how to forgive themselves.

We're not perfect—we have one life and we need to take care of ourselves physically and mentally. We

cannot change other people's thoughts or actions;
we can only show them how we want to be treated.
We have an inner critic, one who tells us about our
mistakes. But once you acknowledge your feelings,
and that critic, you need to give yourself permission
to move on.

She concluded,

People may not deserve your forgiveness, but you
deserve a peaceful mind—one that is free of bad
thoughts—so forgive them and move on. Nothing
good ever comes from revenge. But everything will
come to you when you heal and live in peace.

In other words, don't let that person live rent-free in your head.

The bottom line? Focus on what you can control when things don't go your way or people have wronged you. Try to reframe or forgive. As a result, over the long term, you'll actually feel happier.

Speaking of long term...

PRIORITIZE FUTURE HAPPINESS
Research shows that prioritizing positivity and positive behaviors in the moment is likely to lead to future happiness rather than focusing on happiness itself. This includes helping others, exercising, working to achieve a long-term

goal, building habits that make you healthier, wealthier, and wiser (Haden, 2022).

In short, this involves seeing happiness as a journey, not a destination or a by-product of what you *do*.

Not who you are.

A WORD ABOUT GENETICS

Are some of us destined to be happier than the other? Is it in our DNA? Jolanta Burke, senior lecturer for the Centre for Positive Psychology and Health at RCSI University of Medicine and Health Sciences, writes, "Genetics does not determine who we are, even if it does play a significant role in our wellbeing. What also matters are the choices we make about where we live, who we live with, and how we live our lives, which affect both our happiness and the happiness of the next generations."

In other words, our lives are not made by our DNA or the dreams we dream. It is made by the choices we make. Life is often out of our control. We cannot control what happens outside of us, as much as we want to. But we *can* control our response and the choice about how we look at it. If our vision is a little cloudy, we can get help from our body, mind, and spirit—and our people—to get centered.

Here's to finding joy in the journey.

CHAPTER 12 QUESTIONS:

1. What are the tools/ideas in this book that you will take with you on your journey?

2. Think of a situation where you were upset about how you were not in control of something. How could you reframe your response better?

3. What advice did your parents give you that you didn't first follow, but now do? How has it helped?

4. Do you think some of us are destined to be happier than others? Why or why not?

5. What can you do today to find joy in the journey and prioritize happiness?

Acknowledgments

———

Writing a book is not for the faint of heart. The process was like Jacob in the Old Testament when he wrestled with God. The nature of the content was extremely personal and left me on countless days feeling vulnerable and raw. Spent. I wanted to give up many, many, many times. I felt like I was running the Chicago Marathon, like I did in 2002. But I persevered.

As I worked on completing my book marathon twenty years later, my world was upside down. Historic Supreme Court rulings and mass shootings in my backyard filled the headlines and broke my heart. Three out of five members of my household had COVID-19, including me. My internet stopped working for a week. My dad's health took a turn for the worse. I broke my left wrist and needed surgery. It's been a lot, but the tools I've written about in this book powered me through this chaotic time.

I reached the finish line with the help of my tribe. First and foremost, my husband, who has been my immovable rock. I'm forever grateful for his love and support. Next, my children. They are one of my greatest accomplishments, greatest joys, and the greatest source of my gray hair. Hopefully, they will see the strength and power in sharing your story, even the unattractive parts.

My extended family has also stood by my side through the stories in this book. I'll never forget when my mom, dad, stepmom, mother-in-law, and sister-in-law stayed overnight at the hospital when I lost Faith Lily. They were with me in that deep valley and the others I've since walked through. My siblings and siblings-in-law have also been a pillar of support and strength, loving me unconditionally.

To my friends who are like family—I'm so, so, so blessed to have you in my life. I truly couldn't have written this book without my "board of directors," and my extended network of friends who accept me as I am and have stood by my side at school, work, and in life. I try to give back to my tribe too and hope you have felt my love in return.

I'd also like to thank the brave people who shared their stories with me for this book.

And for my professional team—my therapist, my executive coach, my yoga teacher, and all the fellow authors and people at New Degree Press—thank you for encouraging me along the way to get to the finish line. Eric, Quinn, Angela, Julie, Kyra, Janice and so many more.

Also, a special thanks to all of my friends and family who supported my publishing campaign by donating or helping to spread the word. This book wouldn't be possible without your generosity. These kind souls include:

Abby S., Ada D., Alex S., Allison P., Amanda D. Angela H., Anjali S., Ann B., Audra N., Beth L., Betsy B., Brian H., Bulent A., Carrie C., Carrine B., Catharine S. Chaunda R-S., Cheryl W., Christie L., Christina C., Colette P., Colleen H., Dan K., Dawn L., Deanna T., Deb S., Debbie M., Deborah K., Denise B., Denise N., E.L., Eileen S., Elena I., Eric K., Erica H., Erin T., Gabriela K., Grace K., Heidi H., Janine M., Jeannine B., Jeff L., Jennie B., Jennifer B, Jennifer G., Jennifer S., Jessica M., Jesus R., Joanne C., John B., Julie H. Kari D., Karin W., Karynn K, Kate B., Katherine T-H., Kathleen C., Kathryn H., Katie M., Kelly B., Kelly M., Kim W., Kris G., Krista E., Kristin B., Kristina P-L., Larry Z., Laura B., Laura F., Laura K., Laura M., Laura T-C., Laura W., Lily G., Lisa B. Lisa D., Margaret B., Marian H., Marla E., Martha S., Mary B., Matty M., Maude C., Maura D., Meghan G., Melissa B., Melissa P., Michele K.,, Molly W., Nancy D., Nancy T., Natalie Y., Nate H., Ofelia S., Patricia K., Paul A., Paul P., Hope D., Rachel R., Renee G., Rhonda G, Rico B., Saioa A., Sandy M., Scott B., Sean W., Stacey G., Tamara B., Tara B., Tara C., Ted B., Teresa S., Terry M., Tina R., Trudi P., Valerie J., Valerie W., Vanessa C., Vivian F., Wendy F-H., Wendy K. and Yona S.

Also, thank you, dear reader, for getting this far. If you want to share comments, thoughts, or feedback you can reach me at authortracybaldwin.com.

Last, but not least, there wouldn't be a book without God, the universe, a snowstorm, and Sarah Silverman. Thank you.

Appendix

——

INTRODUCTION

Harvard Medical School. "National Comorbidity Survey (NCS) 2007, Table 2. 12-Month Prevalence of Dsm-Iv/Wmh-Cidi Disorders by Sex and Cohort 1 (N=9282)." August 21, 2017. Retrieved from https://www.hcp.med.harvard.edu/ncs/ index.php. Data Table 2: https://www.hcp.med.harvard.edu/ ncs/ftpdir/table_ncsr_12monthprevgenderxage.pdf

Kessler, Ronald C., et. al. "Lifetime prevalence and age-of-onset distributions of DSM-IV disorders in the National Comorbidity Survey Replication." *Archives of General Psychiatry* 62, no. 6 (2005): 593-602. doi: 10.1001/archpsyc.62.6.593.

Kaiser Family Foundation. "Adults Reporting Symptoms of Anxiety or Depressive Disorder During COVID-19 Pandemic." 2022. https://www.kff.org/other/state-indicator/ adults-reporting-symptoms-of-anxiety-or-depressive-dis-order-during-covid-19-pandemic/?currentTime-frame=0&sortModel=%7B%22colId%22:%22Location%22,-%22sort%22:%22asc%22%7D

Leupp, Katrina. "Even Supermoms Get the Blues: Employment, Gender Attitudes, and Depression." *Society and Mental Health* 8, no. 2 (July 18, 2018): 316-333. https://doi.org/10.1177/2156869318785406

Panchal, Nirmita, Rabah Kamal, Cynthia Cox, and Rachel Garfield. "The Implications of COVID-19 for Mental Health and Substance Use." *Kaiser Family Foundation*, February 10, 2021. https://www.kff.org/coronavirus-covid-19/issue-brief/the-implications-of-covid-19-for-mental-health-and-substance-use/.

CHAPTER 1

American Foundation for Suicide Prevention. "Suicide Statistics." 2022. https://afsp.org/suicide-statistics/.

CDC and Prevention. "Suicide and Self-Harm Injury." 2022. https://www.cdc.gov/nchs/fastats/suicide.htm.

Dolgin, Rebecca. "The Impact Of Covid-19 On Suicide Rates." Remedy Health Media, LLC. 2022. https://www.psycom.net/covid-19-suicide-rates.

Ludlam, Julia. "25 Inspirational Quotes to Celebrate New Beginnings." *Country Living*. January 8, 2020. https://www.countryliving.com/life/g30337217/new-beginnings-quotes/?slide=10

National Weather Service. "January 30-31, 2021: Significant Snowfall Event for Northern Illinois and Northwest Indiana." 2022. https://www.weather.gov/lot/2021jan3031_snow.

SAVE. "Warning Signs of Suicide." 2022. https://save.org/
about-suicide/warning-signs-risk-factors-protective-factors/.

Silverman, Sarah Kate. "Put Suicide off for Tomorrow." *Instagram*, (@sarahkatesilverman). January 29, 2021. https://
www.instagram.com/p/CKpt2D4Ah6h/.

U.S. Bureau of Labor Statistics. "Table 4. Quits levels and rates
by industry and region, seasonally adjusted." June 1, 2022.
https://www.bls.gov/news.release/jolts.t04.htm.

Van Amburg, Jessie. "Why I Quit My Job During the Pandemic,
Like Millions of Other Americans." *Katie Couric Media*,
June 30, 2021. https://katiecouric.com/culture/workplace/
why-i-quit-my-job-during-the-pandemic-like-millions-of-
other-americans/?utm_source=Sailthru&utm_medium=e-
mail&utm_campaign=WUC_Monday&utm_term=all_
users.

World Health Organization. "Burn-out an "occupational phenomenon": International Classification of
Diseases." May 28, 2019. https://www.who.int/news/
item/28-05-2019-burn-out-an-occupational-phenomenon-in-
ternational-classification-of-diseases#:~:text=%E2%80%9C-
Burn%2Dout%20is%20a%20syndrome,related%20to%20
one%27s%20job%3B%20and.

World Health Organization. "COVID-19 pandemic triggers 25%
increase in prevalence of anxiety and depression worldwide."
2022. https://www.who.int/news/item/02-03-2022-covid-19-
pandemic-triggers-25-increase-in-prevalence-of-anxiety-
and-depression-worldwide.

U.S. Department of Labor. "Family and Medical Leave Act." 2022. https://www.dol.gov/agencies/whd/fmla.

CHAPTER 2

Döpfner, Mathias. "Jeff Bezos reveals what it's like to build an empire—and why he's willing to spend $1 billion a year to fund the most important mission of his life." *Business Insider,* April 28, 2018. https://www. businessinsider.com/jeff-bezos-interview-axel-springer-ceo-amazon-trump-blue-origin-family-regulation-washington-post-2018-4.

Feliciano, Niro. *This Book Won't Make You Happy: Eight Keys to Finding True Contentment.* Minneapolis: Broadleaf, 2022.

Goodreads. *Fred Rogers - Quotes.* 2022. https://www.goodreads.com/author/quotes/32106.Fred_Rogers.

Marsico, Sandy. Founder & CEO, Sandstorm®. 2022. https://www.linkedin.com/in/usabilityexpert/.

Martino, Jessica, Jennifer Pegg, and Elizabeth Pegg Frates, MD. "The Connection Prescription: Using the Power of Social Interactions and the Deep Desire for Connectedness to Empower Health and Wellness." *American Journal of Lifestyle Medicine* 11, no. 6 (2017 Nov-Dec): 466–475. doi: 10.1177/1559827615608788.

Mineo, Liz. "Good Genes Are Nice, But Joy Is Better." *Harvard Gazette,* April 11, 2017. https://news.harvard.edu/gazette/

story/2017/04/over-nearly-80-years-harvard-study-has-been-showing-how-to-live-a-healthy-and-happy-life/.

Pesce, Nicole Lyn. "Jeff Bezos praises his dad's 'grit and determination in immigrating to America as a teen." *MarketWatch,* May 17, 2019. https://www.marketwatch.com/story/jeff-bezos-praises-his-dads-grit-and-determination-in-immigrating-to-america-as-a-teen-2019-05-17.

Quinn, Rybecca. "Was Jeff Bezos Born Rich? (Everything To Know)." *The Cold Wire.* 2022. https://www.thecoldwire.com/was-jeff-bezos-born-rich/.

Rosoff, Matt. "Jeff Bezos Told What May Be the Best Startup Investment Story Ever." *Business Insider,* October 20, 2016. https://www.businessinsider.com/jeff-bezos-on-early-amazon-investors-2016-10.

Waldinger, Robert. "What Makes A Good Life? Lessons From The Longest Study On Happiness." Filmed December 2015 at TEDx Beacon Street, Brookline, MA. Video, 12:38.

Zimmer, Benjamin. "Figurative "Bootstraps" (1834)." https://listserv.linguistlist.org/pipermail/ads-l/2005-August/052756.html.

CHAPTER 3

Ahmad, MPH1, Farida B.; Robert N. Anderson, PhD2. "The Leading Causes of Death in the US for 2020." *JAMA*, 325, no. 18 (2021):1829-1830. doi:10.1001/jama.2021.5469.

Bowler, Kate. *No Cure for Being Human: And Other Truths I Need to Hear.* New York City: Random House, 2021.

Cassella, Megan. "The Pandemic Drove Women Out of The Workforce. Will They Come Back?" *Politico*, July 22, 2021. https://www.politico.com/news/2021/07/22/coronavirus-pandemic-women-workforce-500329.

Cuddy, Amy, JillEllyn Riley. "Why This Stage of the Pandemic Makes Us So Anxious: Many of Us Are Suffering From 'Pandemic Flux Syndrome.'" *Washington Post,* August 11, 2021. https://www.washingtonpost.com/outlook/2021/08/11/pandemic-anxiety-psychology-delta/.

FBI. "NICS Firearm Checks: Top 10 Highest Days/Weeks." 2022. https://www.fbi.gov/file-repository/nics_firearm_checks_top_10_highest_days_weeks.pdf/view.

Feiler, Bruce. *Life in the Transitions.* London: Penguin Press, 2020.

Fisher, Jen. "Workplace Burnout Survey: Burnout Without Borders." Deloitte. 2018. https://www2.deloitte.com/us/en/pages/about-deloitte/articles/burnout-survey.html.

Gallup. "State of the Global Workplace: 2022 Report." 2022. https://www.gallup.com/workplace/349484/state-of-the-global-workplace.aspx#ite-350777.

Gottlieb, Lori. "'Happiness as a Byproduct of Living Our Lives in a Meaningful Way Is What We All Aspire To, but Happiness as the Goal Is a Recipe for Disaster.' Why I dumped the happiness book to write #MaybeYouShouldTalkToSomeone. my convo w @arthurbrooks @theatlantic http://bit.ly/3AQP-TUu." *Twitter @LoriGottlieb1,* September 29, 2021. https://twitter.com/LoriGottlieb1/status/1443233917562142724.

Haelle, Tara. "Your 'Surge Capacity' Is Depleted—It's Why You Feel Awful." August 17, 2020. https://elemental.medium.com/your-surge-capacity-is-depleted-it-s-why-you-feel-awful-de285d542f4c.

Iacurci, Greg. "Unemployment Is Nearing Great Depression Levels. Here's How the Eras Are Similar—and Different." May 19, 2020. https://www.cnbc.com/2020/05/19/unemployment-today-vs-the-great-depression-how-do-the-eras-compare.html.

Iati, Marisa, Lindsey Bever and Paulina Firozi. "Millions of Workers Are Quitting Their Jobs During the Pandemic." *Washington Post,* June 17, 2021. https://www.washingtonpost.com/business/2021/06/17/record-workers-quit-pandemic/.

Johns Hopkins Healthcare Solution. "What's the Cost of the Mind-Body Connection?" 2022. https://www.johnshopkinssolutions.com/cost-of-the-mind-body-connection/.

Ludlam, Julia. "25 Inspirational Quotes to Celebrate New Beginnings: Welcome to a Brand-new You." *Country Living.* January 8, 2020. https://www.countryliving.com/life/g30337217/new-beginnings-quotes/?slide=16.

MacFarquhar, Neil. "Murders Spiked in 2020 in Cities Across the United States." *New York Times.* Septem-

ber 27, 2021. https://www.nytimes.com/2021/09/27/us/
fbi-murders-2020-cities.html?campaign_id=60&em-
c=edit_na_20210927&instance_id=0&nl=break-
ing-news&ref=cta&regi_id=62676758&segment_
id=70018&user_id=744d08627f24f313c0490bc1aba0cbe3.

Mekouar, Dora. "Why Homicide Rates in US Spiked 30%
During COVID Pandemic." *VOA News*, 2022. https://www.
voanews.com/a/why-homicide-rates-spiked-30-during-the-
pandemic-/6420391.html.

McKinsey. "Women in the Workplace." September 27, 2021.
https://www.mckinsey.com/featured-insights/diversi-
ty-and-inclusion/women-in-the-workplace.

Milkman, Katy. *How to Change: The Science of Getting from
Where You Are to Where You Want to Be*. London: Penguin
Group, 2021.

SHRM. "Interactive Chart: How Historic Has the Great
Resignation Been?" 2022. https://www.shrm.org/
resourcesandtools/hr-topics/talent-acquisition/pages/inter-
active-quits-level-by-year.aspx.

Skipper, Clay. "Why Simply Hustling Harder Won't Help You
With the Big Problems in Life: A Conversation With Author
and Self-Help Historian Kate Bowler About How Productivity Culture Is a Lot Like a Religion." *GQ*. September 24, 2021.
https://www.gq.com/story/kate-bowler-hustle-culture?utm_
source=onsite-share&utm_medium=email&utm_cam-
paign=onsite-share&utm_brand=gq.

Snower, Dennis. "Awakening in the Post-pandemic World." *Brookings* (blog) March 27, 2020. https://www.brookings.edu/blog/future-development/2020/03/27/awakening-in-the-post-pandemic-world/.

The Lancet Covid-19 Commission. "Mental Health & Wellbeing." 2022. https://covid19commission.org/mental-health-wellbeing.

Threlkeld, Kristy. "Employee Burnout Report: COVID-19's Impact and 3 Strategies to Curb It." *Indeed*, March 11, 2021. https://www.indeed.com/lead/preventing-employee-burnout-report.

WebMD Editorial Contributors. "Burnout: Symptoms and Signs." *WebMD*. 2020. https://www.webmd.com/mental-health/burnout-symptoms-signs#:~:text=Burnout%20is%20a%20form.

CHAPTER 4

Bonanno, G. A. "Loss, Trauma, and Human Resilience: Have We Underestimated the Human Capacity to Thrive After Extremely Aversive Events?" *American Psychologist* 59, no. 1 (2004): 20–28. https://doi.org/10.1037/0003-066X.59.1.20.

Brody, M.P.H., Debra J. and Qiuping Gu, M.D., Ph.D. "Antidepressant Use Among Adults: United States, 2015-2018." CDC. September 2020. https://www.cdc.gov/nchs/products/databriefs/db377.htm.

Doctor Neha. "TEDx Berkeley The Communication Cure."
    February 26, 2012. Video, 20:16. Accessed June 17, 2022. 20:16
    https://www.youtube.com/watch?v=BDTG2mJUqho&t=778s.

Gordon M.D., James S. *Unstuck: Your Guide to the Seven-Stage
    Journey Out of Depression.* London: Penguin Books, 2008.

Johns Hopkins Healthcare Solution. "What's the Cost of the
    Mind-Body Connection?" 2022. https://www.johnshopkins-
    solutions.com/cost-of-the-mind-body-connection/.

Medical News Today. "Everything You Need to Know About
    Chemical Imbalances in the Brain." 2019. https://www.medi-
    calnewstoday.com/articles/326475.

Singer, Michael. *Untethered Soul.* Oakland; New Harbinger,
    2022.

van der Kolk, MD, Bessel. *The Body Keeps Score: Mind, Brain
    and Body in the Transformation of Trauma.* London: Pen-
    guin, 2014.

Witters, Dan and Sangeeta Agrawal. "Americans' Life Ratings
    Reach Record High." *Gallup,* 2021. https://news.gallup.com/
    poll/351932/americans-life-ratings-reach-record-high.aspx.

CHAPTER 5

Atlas, James. "Really, You're Not in a Book Club?" *The New York
    Times,* March 22, 2014. https://www.nytimes.com/2014/03/23/
    opinion/sunday/really-youre-not-in-a-book-club.html

"Book Clubs by the Numbers." *BookBrowse.com.* March 22, 2014.https://www.bookbrowse.com/blogs/editor/index. cfm/2014/3/25/Book-Clubs-by-The-Numbers

Burger, Pamela. "Women's Groups and the Rise of the Book Club. The History of the Book Club." *Daily JSTOR,* August 12, 2015. https://daily.jstor.org/feature-book-club/.

Goldberg, Joel. "It Takes A Village to Determine the Origins of an African Proverb." *NPR,* July 30, 2016. https://www.npr. org/sections/goatsandsoda/2016/07/30/487925796/it-takes-a-village-to-determine-the-origins-of-an-african-proverb.

Grosberg, Denise, Ryan Merlin, and Paul J. Zak. "What Makes Women Happy: Oxytocin Release Correlates with Life Satisfaction." Docplayer. https://docplayer. net/36144155-What-makes-women-happy-oxytocin-release-correlates-with-life-satisfaction-denise-grosberg-ryan-merlin-and-paul-j-zak.html.

Haden, Jeff. "This 2,000-Year-Old Philosophy Reveals 4 Timeless Ways to Be More Likable (and Successful): Because Nice People Can Finish First." *Inc.* 2022. https://www.inc.com/jeff-haden/this-2000-year-old-philosophy-reveals-4-timeless-ways-to-be-more-likable-and-successful.html.

LaRosa, John, "$10.4 Billion Self-Improvement Market Pivots to Virtual Delivery During the Pandemic." *MarketResearch. com*, August 2, 2021. Marketresearch.com (blog). https://blog.marketresearch.com/10.4-billion-self-improvement-market-pivots-to-virtual-delivery-during-the-pandemic.

McHugh, Jess. "How Women Invented Book Clubs, Revolution-izing Reading and Their Own Lives More Than 150 Years Before Oprah And Reese Witherspoon, Women Began Reading Together In Groups." *Washington Post*, March 27, 2021. https://www.washingtonpost.com/history/2021/03/27/womens-book-clubs-history-oprah-reese/.

NPD. "Self Help Book Sales are Rising Fast in the US, The NPD Group Says." January 13, 2020. https://www.npd.com/news/press-releases/2020/self-help-book-sales-are-rising-fast-in-the-us-the-npd-group-says/.

CHAPTER 6

Albom, Mitch. "Katie Couric and I are talking! Welcomed Katie, author of the #1 *New York Times* bestselling memoir, "Going There," for a wide-ranging conversation on journalism, faith, love and loss, being vulnerable and putting positivity out in the world -- in words and actions! Tune in and be impressed that this is the first time I've invited a "guest" into a live stream. #live #goingthere #strangerinthelifeboat #positivity #newrelease #bestsellers." *Instagram, @mitchalbom.* November 5, 2021. https://www.instagram.com/tv/CV5eZCTJy7a/.

APA Dictionary of Psychology. "Yin and Yang." 2022. https://dictionary.apa.org/yin-and-yang.

Beck, Marth. "Martha Beck: How to Tell When the Universe Is Sending You Signs." *Oprah.* 2022. https://www.oprah.com/inspiration/martha-beck-how-to-tell-when-the-universe-is-sending-you-signs.

CNN. "Adele gets candid on weight and divorce in Oprah interview." November 15, 2021. Video, 4:43 https://www.youtube.com/watch?v=KbejihtqvCs.

John Hopkins Medicine. "Ayurveda." 2022. https://www.hopkinsmedicine.org/health/wellness-and-prevention/ayurveda.

Lawrence, Brother. *Practicing the Presence of God.* New Kensington: Whitaker House: 1982.

Leland, Karen. "Labyrinths: Ancient Aid for Modern Stresses." *WedMD.* 2022 https://www.webmd.com/balance/features/labyrinths-for-modern-stresses.

Madeson, Ph.D., Melissa. "Embodiment Practices: How to Heal Through Movement." *Positive Psychology,* August 11, 2021. https://positivepsychology.com/embodiment-philosophy-practices/.

Rose, Sahara. "Dharma Archetype Quiz." 2021. https://www.dharmaarchetypequiz.com/dharma-archetype-quiz/.

Shetty, Jay. *Think Like a Monk: Train Your Mind for Peace and Purpose Every Day.* New York City: Simon & Schuster, 2020.

CHAPTER 7

Bajracharya, Srizu. "The Tale of the Singing Bowl." *Kathmandu Post,* September 14, 2019. https://kathmandupost.com/art-culture/2019/08/14/the-tale-of-the-singing-bowl.

Bauer, M.D., Brent A. "What Are the Benefits of Aromatherapy? *Mayo Clinic,* June 6, 2020. https://www.mayoclinic.org/ healthy-lifestyle/consumer-health/expert-answers/aroma-therapy/faq-20058566.

Breen, Kerry. "Simone Biles says she's 'keeping the door open' for Olympic return." *NBC News,* August 4, 2021. https:// www.nbcnews.com/news/olympics/simone-biles-says-she-s-leaving-door-open-olympic-return-n1275905.

Buchholz, Katharina. "The Most Popular Yoga and Mindfulness Apps, Yoga and Meditation." *Statista,* June 21, 2021. https:// www.statista.com/chart/22059/most-popular-yoga-and-med-itation-apps/.

Cameron, Julia. *The Artist's Way, A Spiritual Path to Higher Creativity.* New York City: J.P. Tarcher/Putnam, 2002.

Goldberg, Natalie. *Writing Down the Bones: Freeing the Writer Within.* Boulder: Shambhala, 2016.

Goldsby, PhD, Tamara L., Michael E. Goldsby, PhD, Mary McWalters, BA, and Paul J. Mills, PhD. "Effects of Singing Bowl Sound Meditation on Mood, Tension, and Well-being: An Observational Study." *Evidence Based Complementary Alternative Medicine,* 22 no. 3 (July 2017): 401–406. doi: 10.1177/2156587216668109.

Grandview Research. "Aromatherapy Diffusers Market Size, Share & Trends Analysis Report By Product (Ultrasonic, Nebulizer, Evaporative, Heat), By Application, By Distribu-tion, By Region, And Segment Forecasts, 2020 - 2027." 2022.

https://www.grandviewresearch.com/industry-analysis/aro-
matherapy-diffusers-market.

Louv, Richard. *Last Child in the Woods: Saving Our Children
from Nature Deficit Disorder.* Chapel Hill: Algonquin Books,
2005.

Rrakicevic, Mira. "27 Meditation Statistics for Your Well-Being
in 2022." *DisturbMeNot! Sleep Better,* January 3, 2022. https://
disturbmenot.co/meditation-statistics/

Ryan, Maggie. "If Your Thoughts Race at Night, Sleep
Meditations Can Help Calm Your Mind." *Yahoo Lifestyle,* September 29, 2021. https://www.yahoo.com/
lifestyle/did-10-minute-sleep-meditations-145956096.
html?guccounter=1&guce_referrer=aHR0cHM6Ly93d-
3cuZ29vZ2xlLmNvbS8&guce_referrer_sig=AQAAAB-
Do6Ke2wVQDXc9qylZDXW2hFTmd4oi-IOSigj9uehE_
hWiic77j7HTzUyWgaybe8vW7nRBoBwoH8aT8IstxFqf-
gydMNCWwqIYWExwo1yqzr4eFvochGewO_GZdjO-
8Qf3Xs3hoVYK4yaDuPb6Sgrk942pgTSZ58-3uKH5bGsZY3k.

Singer, Michael. *Untethered Soul.* Oakland: New Harbinger,
2022.

Sparks, Dana. "Home Remedies: What are the benefits
of aromatherapy?" *Mayo Clinic,* May 8, 2019. https://
newsnetwork.mayoclinic.org/discussion/home-reme-
dies-what-are-the-benefits-of-aromatherapy/

The Good Body. 27 Meditation Statistics: Data and Trends Revealed for 2022. 2022. https://www.thegoodbody.com/meditation-statistics/.

CHAPTER 8

APA. "What is Cognitive Behavioral Therapy?" 2022. https://www.apa.org/ptsd-guideline/patients-and-families/cognitive-behavioral.

Beck, Julie. "The Six Forces That Fuel Friendship." *The Atlantic*, June 10, 2022. https://www.theatlantic.com/family/archive/2022/06/six-ways-make-maintain-friends/661232/?utm_source=newsletter&utm_medium=e-mail&utm_campaign=atlantic-daily-newsletter&utm_content=20220610&utm_term=The%20Atlantic%20Daily.

Brown, Brené. "The Power of Vulnerability." Filmed at Houston TEDx, December 23, 2010. https://www.ted.com/talks/brene_brown_the_power_of_vulnerability?language=en

Chatterje, Rhitu. "The new 988 mental health hotline is live. Here's what to know." *NPR*, July 16, 2022. https://www.npr.org/sections/health-shots/2022/07/15/1111316589/988-suicide-hotline-number

Crowley, Mark. "Remote Work Has a Downside. Here's Why I Want to Go Back to the Office." *Fast Company*, November 30, 2021. https://www.fastcompany.com/90700878/remote-work-has-a-downside-heres-why-i-want-to-go-back-to-the-office.

DiJulio, Bianca, Liz Hamel, Cailey Muñana, and Molivann Brodie. "Loneliness and Social Isolation in the United States, the United Kingdom, and Japan: An International Survey." *Kaiser Family Foundation*, August 30, 2018. https://www.kff.org/other/report/loneliness-and-social-isolation-in-the-united-states-the-united-kingdom-and-japan-an-international-survey/

Glantz, Jen. "I Hired a Friendship Coach to Help Me Make Friends. Here's What Happened." *NBC News*, February 24, 2020. https://www.nbcnews.com/better/lifestyle/i-hired-friendship-coach-help-me-make-friends-here-s-ncna1141571.

Raypole, Crystal. "Six Ways Friendship is Good for Your Health." *Healthline*, August 17, 2020. https://www.healthline.com/health/benefits-of-friendship

Hofmann, Ph.D., Stefan G., Anu Asnaani, M.A., Imke J.J. Vonk, M.A., Alice T. Sawyer, M.A., and Angela Fang, M.A. "The Efficacy of Cognitive Behavioral Therapy: A Review of Meta-analyses." *Cognitive Therapy and Research*. 36, No. 5 (2012): 427–440. doi: 10.1007/s10608-012-9476-1.

Holt-Lunstad, Julianne, Timothy B. Smith, Mark Baker, Tyler Harris, David Stephenson. "Loneliness and Social Isolation as Risk Factors for Mortality: A Meta-Analytic Review." Brigham Young University. March 23, 2015. https://scholarsarchive.byu.edu/cgi/viewcontent.cgi?article=3024&context=facpub.

International Coaching Federation. "Empowering the World Through Coaching." 2022. https://coachingfederation.org.

John Hopkins Medicine. "Ayurveda." 2022. https://www.hop-kinsmedicine.org/health/wellness-and-prevention/ayurveda.

Jones, Valerie K., Michael Hanus, Changmin Yan, Marcia Y. Shade, Julie B. Boron, Rafael M. Bicudo. "Reducing Lone-liness Among Aging Adults: The Roles of Personal Voice Assistants and Anthropomorphic Interactions." *Frontiers in Public Health*, December 10, 2021. https://doi.org/10.3389/fpubh.2021.750736

Keisler-Starkey, Katherine and Lisa N. Bunch. "Health Insurance Coverage in the United States: 2020." September 14, 2021. https://www.census.gov/library/publications/2021/demo/p60-274.html.

LaMotte, Sandee. "How to Become More Resilient, According to the Research." *CNN*, December 7, 2021. https://www.cnn.com/2021/12/07/health/resilience-tips-wellness/index.html.

Levy, John. *You're Invited: The Art and Science of Cultivating Influence.* New York: Harper Business, 2021.

Murthy, Dr. Vivek H. *Together: The Healing Power of Human Connection in a Sometimes Lonely World.* London: Harper Wave, 2021.

Natale, Nicol. "Denise Austin Shares Her Best Tips for Beating Menopause-Induced Mood Swings." *Prevention,* October 13, 2021. https://www.prevention.com/health/a37912643/denise-austin-menopause-tips/.

Newland, Stephen. "The Power of Accountability." *Association for Financial Counseling & Planning Education*, Third Quarter 2018. https://www.afcpe.org/news-and-publications/the-standard/2018-3/the-power-of-accountability/

Southwick, Steven M., Dennis S. Charney. *Resilience: The Science of Mastering Life's Greatest Challenges* 1st Edition. Cambridge: Cambridge University Press, 2012.

Steimer, Sarah. "How Do Cities Impact Mental Health? A New Study Finds Lower Rates of Depression." *UChicago News*, July 28, 2021. https://news.uchicago.edu/story/cities-depression-lower-rates-mental-health-psychology-socioeconomic-networks.

Szmigiera, M. "Biggest Companies in the World By Market Capitalization 2021." *Statista*, September 10, 2021. https://www.statista.com/statistics/263264/top-companies-in-the-world-by-market-capitalization/.

Thompson, Derek. "The Great Resignation Is Accelerating: A Lasting Effect of This Pandemic Will Be a Revolution in Worker Expectations." *The Atlantic*, October 15, 2021. https://www.theatlantic.com/ideas/archive/2021/10/great-resignation-accelerating/620382/.

van Harmelen, A.-L., R. A. Kievit, K. Ioannidis, S. Neufeld, P. B. Jones, E. Bullmore, R. Dolan, P. Fonagy, I. Goodyer and The NSPN Consortium. "Adolescent Friendships Predict Later Resilient Functioning Across Psychosocial Domains In A Healthy Community Cohort." *Cambridge University Press*, April 11, 2017. https://www.cambridge.org/core/

journals/psychological-medicine/article/adolescent-friend-
ships-predict-later-resilient-functioning-across-psy-
chosocial-domains-in-a-healthy-community-cohort/
E8D06DC512C7A0EC720FF767F9E44504.

Weiner, Stacy. "Addressing the Escalating Psychiatrist Shortage."
AAMC. February 12, 2018. https://www.aamc.org/news-in-
sights/addressing-escalating-psychiatrist-shortage.

Welch, Edward T. *When People are Big and God is Small.* Phil-
lipsburg: P&R Publishing, 1997.

Young, Molly. "The Reigning Queen of Pandemic Yoga." *New
York Times,* November 25, 2020. https://www.nytimes.
com/2020/11/25/magazine/yoga-adriene-mishler.html.

CHAPTER 9

Dubey, Amartansh. "What did Nikola Tesla mean by his quote,
if you wish to understand the universe, think of energy,
frequency and vibration?" *Quora.* 2022. https://www.quora.
com/What-did-Nikola-Tesla-mean-by-his-quote-if-you-
wish-to-understand-the-universe-think-of-energy-frequen-
cy-and-vibration.

History.com editors. "Nikola Tesla." *History,* March 13, 2020.
https://www.history.com/topics/inventions/nikola-tesla

Mayo Clinic Staff. "Positive thinking: Stop negative self-talk to
reduce stress." *Mayo Clinic.* 2022. "https://www.mayoclinic.
org/healthy-lifestyle/stress-management/in-depth/posi-
tive-thinking/art-20043950.

CHAPTER 10

Elsie. "How to Create Margin in Your Life for a Simpler Schedule (2 Methods That Work)." *Richly Rooted,* January 6, 2014. https://richlyrooted.com/2014/01/create-margin-in-your-life-for-a-simpler-schedule.html.

Gandhi, Mahatma and Krishna Kripalani. *All Men are Brothers: Autobiographical Reflections,* London: Bloomsbury Academic, 2005.

Gollwitzer, Peter M. "Implementation Intentions: Strong Effects of Simple Plans." *American Psychologist* 54 no. 7 (1999): 493-503. DOI:10.1037/0003-066X.54.7.493.

Gusau, Murtadha. "The Importance of Forgiveness in Islam." *Premium Times.* February 12, 2021. https://www.premiumtimesng.com/opinion/442363-the-importance-of-forgiveness-in-islam-by-murtadha-gusau.html.

Johns Hopkins Medicine. "Vital Signs (Body Temperature, Pulse Rate, Respiration Rate, Blood Pressure)." 2022. https://www.hopkinsmedicine.org/health/conditions-and-diseases/vital-signs-body-temperature-pulse-rate-respiration-rate-blood-pressure.

Ludlam, Julia. "25 Inspirational Quotes to Celebrate New Beginnings: Welcome to a Brand-new You." *Country Living,* January 8, 2020. https://www.countryliving.com/life/g30337217/new-beginnings-quotes/?slide=23.

Moffitt, Phillip. "Forgiving the Unforgivable." *Dharma Wisdom* (blog). 2022. https://dharmawisdom.org/forgiving-the-unforgivable/.

U.S. Centers for Disease Control and Prevention. "Working Together to Reduce Black Maternal Mortality." April 6, 2022. https://www.cdc.gov/healthequity/features/maternal-mortality/index.html

CHAPTER 11

Cleveland Clinic. "What Is Reiki, And Does It Really Work? Here's How This Energy-Healing Practice Can Help Balance You." 2022. https://health.clevelandclinic.org/reiki/.

Kuzmic, Kristina. "Real Talk." *Instagram @kristinakuzmic*, June 28, 2022. https://www.instagram.com/p/CfXaXEZumwN/

O'Donohue, John. *To Bless the Space Between Us: A Book of Blessings*. New York: Doubleday, 2008.

Okura, Lynn. "Maya Angelou: 'Every Age, I've Been Grateful.'" *Huffington Post*, September 4, 2013. https://www.huffpost.com/entry/maya-angelou-age-oprah_n_3862308

CHAPTER 12

Burke, Jolanta." Why Some People Find It Harder to Be Happy, According to Science." *Science Alert,* November 29, 2021. https://www.sciencealert.com/why-some-people-find-it-harder-to-be-happy-according-to-science.

Catalino, Lahnna I.,Algoe, Sara B.,Fredrickson, Barbara L. "Prioritizing Positivity: An Effective Approach to Pursuing Happiness?" *Emotion*, 14 no. 6 (December 2014): 1155-1161. https://psycnet.apa.org/buy/2014-48826-003.

Haden, Jeff. "This 2,000-Year-Old Philosophy Reveals 4 Timeless Ways to Be More Likable (and Successful) Because nice people can finish first." *Inc.*, June 11, 2021. https://www.inc.com/jeff-haden/this-2000-year-old-philosophy-reveals-4-timeless-ways-to-be-more-likable-and-successful.html.

Haden, Jeff. "Want to Be Happier? Science Says 2 Overlooked Variables Can Be the Keys to Happiness: Don't overthink it." *Inc.*, November 16, 2021. https://www.inc.com/jeff-haden/how-to-be-happier-toxic-positivity-fulfillment-emotional-diversity-research-shows-2-key-variables-to-happiness.html.

Hayes, Darren. "I Was One of the Most Famous Pop Stars in the World. No One Knew the Secret Pain I Hid." *Huffington Post,* July 1, 2022. https://www.huffpost.com/entry/darren-hayes-savage-garden-secrets-depression-gay_n_62bb-37c9e4b094be76a90714

Kachroo-Levine, Maya. "47 Anthony Bourdain Quotes That Will Inspire You to Travel More, Eat Better, and Enjoy Life." *Travel and Leisure*, February 5, 2019. https://www.travelandleisure.com/travel-tips/celebrity-travel/anthony-bourdain-travel-food-quotes#:~:text=%E2%80%9CTravel%20isn%27t%20always%20pretty,But%20that%27s%20okay.